CHATHAM'S MILITARY HERITAGE

Clive Holden

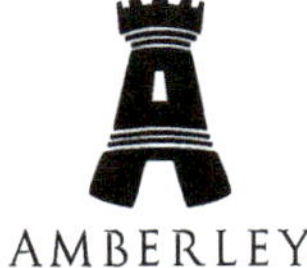

AMBERLEY

First published 2018

Amberley Publishing
The Hill, Stroud
Gloucestershire, GL5 4EP

www.amberley-books.com

Copyright © Clive Holden, 2018

Logo source material courtesy of Gerry van Tonder

The right of Clive Holden to be identified as the
Author of this work has been asserted in accordance
with the Copyrights, Designs and Patents Act 1988.

ISBN 978 1 4456 7422 3 (print)
ISBN 978 1 4456 7423 0 (ebook)

British Library Cataloguing in Publication Data.
A catalogue record for this book is available from the
British Library.

Origination by Amberley Publishing.
Printed in Great Britain.

Contents

Introduction

Chatham lies on a bend of one of the lower reaches of the River Medway in Kent, around 12 miles from its confluence with the Thames. For over 400 years it played a crucial role in the defence of Britain.

Of course, Chatham will always be most famous for its connections with the Royal Navy but the army also maintained a strong presence here, initially to provide defence for the dockyard but later to become one of the country's largest military garrisons and an important training establishment in its own right.

The development of Chatham over the centuries into a major naval and military base extended beyond the town itself. Following the huge expansion of Chatham Dockyard in the last half of the nineteenth century a far greater area of the yard lay within the boundaries of Gillingham than it did Chatham. The defences also expanded way beyond the town, into neighbouring Rochester and Gillingham and across the Medway onto the Hoo Peninsula.

By the turn of the twentieth century the 'Chatham District', as it became known in military terms, was firmly established with the expanded dockyard, the gun wharf, the fortifications of the 'Chatham Lines', the outer ring forts, numerous barracks and the ordnance depots at Chattenden, Upnor and Lodge Hill. It could even boast its own railways. The Dockyard Branch, built in 1877, connected the extensive rail networks within the dockyard and Gun Wharf to the London, Chatham & Dover Railway's main line while over on Hoo the Admiralty operated the Chattenden & Upnor Railway and the Chattenden Naval Tramway.

As well as thousands of service personnel, the military establishment at Chatham employed almost as many civilian workers, the vast majority drawn from the local population of the Medway Towns. When electric trams came to Chatham and Gillingham in the early twentieth century they revolutionised the commute for the local population. The tram network eventually extended into Rainham, Rochester, Strood and Borstal. Fares were deliberately kept low to suit the huge volume of servicemen and dockyard workers who travelled on it.

Chatham's contribution to the nation's efforts in the two world wars can never be forgotten. The dockyard built, repaired and refitted hundreds of vessels of all types, which then went on to serve with the various fleets of the Royal Navy and thousands of servicemen received their basic training here before being posted to theatres of war around the globe.

From the end of the Second World War Chatham's military establishment went into slow decline but continued to make a valuable contribution to the United Kingdom's defence. Although much reduced, that contribution continues to this day with the work of the prestigious Royal School of Military Engineering.

I've written this book not just as a story of Chatham's long military history but as a celebration of its rich military heritage, the evidence of which can still be seen there today.

Clive Holden, May 2018

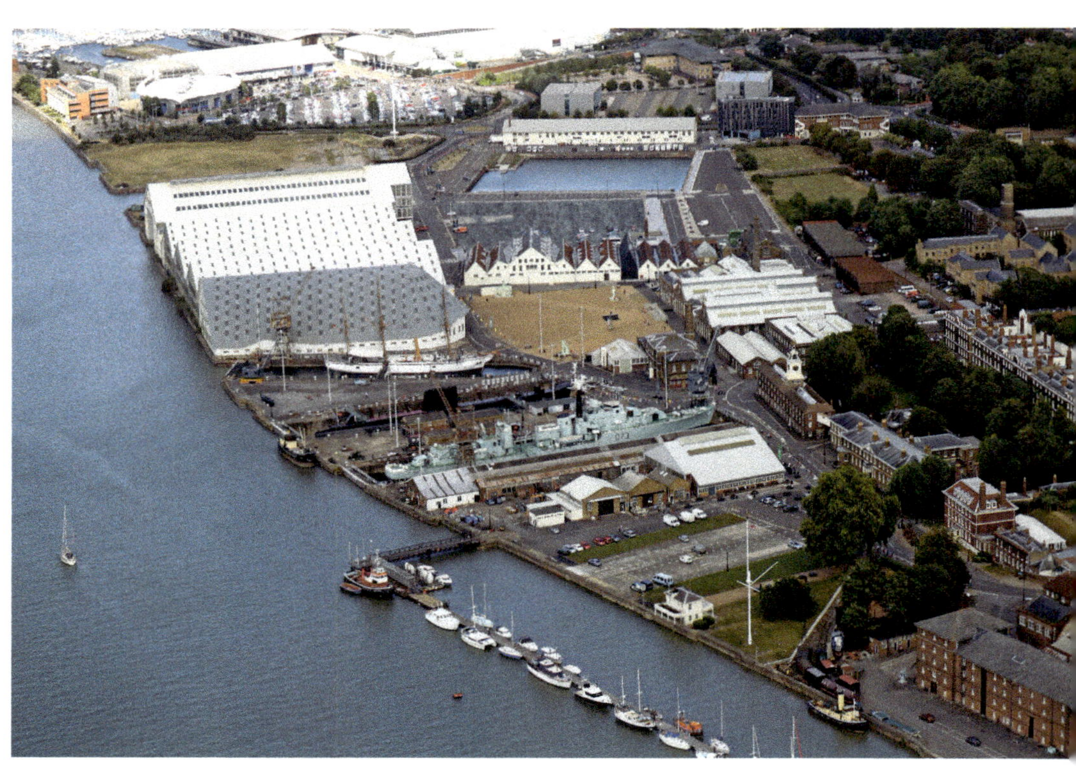

1. Early Times and the Genesis of a Dockyard

Chatham has a rich military heritage dating back to the Roman occupation. It stands on the A2 road, an ancient route named by the Anglo-Saxons as Watling Street, to the south of Rochester. The route was improved by the Romans and became their main line of communication from their port at Richborough on the Kent coast, through Canterbury, over the Medway at Rochester onwards to London. Remains of a Roman military building on the high ground above the town were discovered during the construction of Amherst Redoubt in 1779. Following the Battle of Aylesford in AD 455, this same strategic high ground was occupied by one of the victorious Jutish warlike tribes, the Ceatta, from which the town takes its name.

In the reign of Edward the Confessor, Chatham was in the possession of Godwin, Earl of Kent. After his death, it descended to his eldest son, Harold, later King of England, who was slain at the Battle of Hastings.

After the Norman Conquest of 1066 and the occupation of the throne of England by William, Duke of Normandy, the Hundred of Chatham and Gillingham was awarded by William to his half-brother, Odo, Bishop of Bayeux. In 1082, Odo was involved in a conspiracy against William, who had him arrested and imprisoned in the castle at

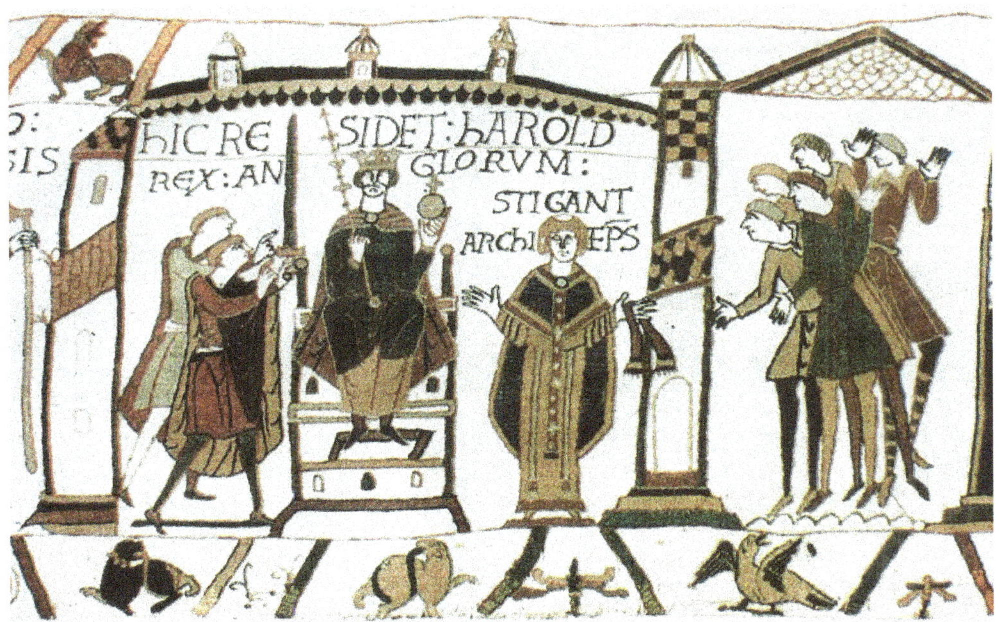

King Harold as depicted in the Bayeux Tapestry.

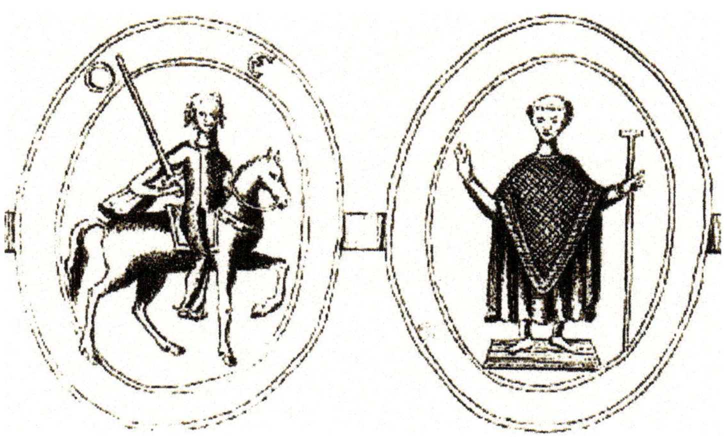

The Seal of Bishop Odo.

Rouen. His lands were confiscated by the Crown and the Barony of Chatham was handed to Hamon de Crevecoeur, another of William's favourites. However, the Normans occupied a hostile country whose indigenous population resented their presence and were prone to violent action against those who oppressed them. It was a common occurrence for Normans to be killed as they went about their business, particularly at night. William ordered a curfew in every village, which ran from eight o'clock till dawn each evening, causing even more resentment among the Saxon population. The Normans, fearful of their safety, eventually retreated behind the walls of their massive

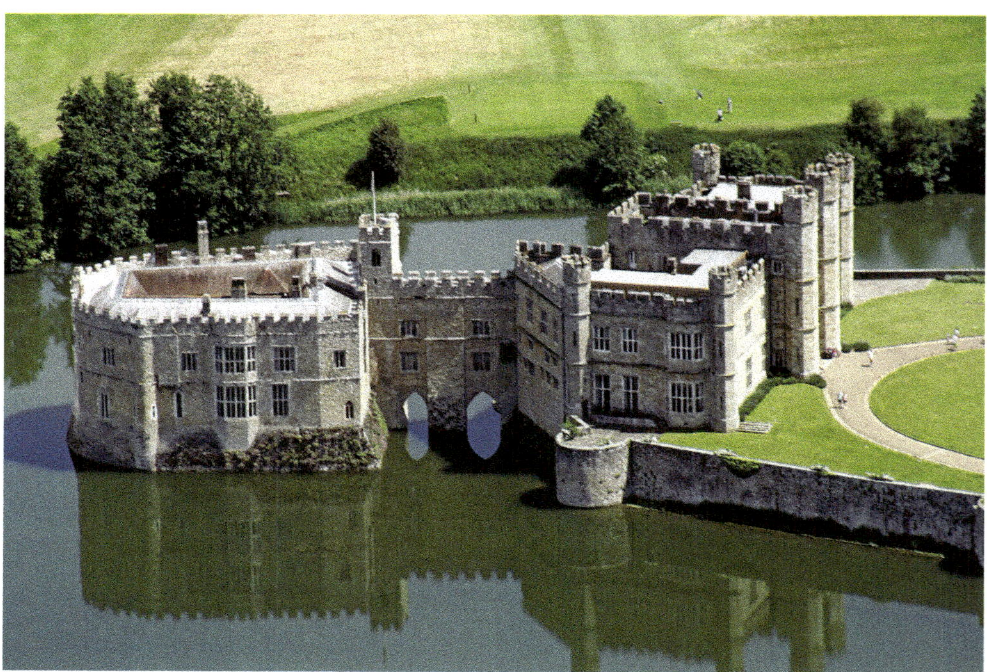

Leeds Castle.

stone castles. One such castle was Leeds Castle, built on the River Len near Maidstone in 1119 by Robert, grandson of Hamon de Crevecoeur, and it was around this time that the family removed themselves from Chatham and became the parish's absentee landlords. Around 1130 the family bestowed upon the Priory of Black Canons at Leeds the church and all the profits of the parish of Chatham with 30 acres of land together with all its liberties and appurtenances.

The barony and manor of Chatham remained in the Crevecoeur family until 1264 when Robert Creuker, thrice great-grandson of Robert de Crevecoeur, took part in Simon de Montfort's failed rebellion against Henry III after which Chatham and Creuker's other estates were seized by the Crown. Robert was later restored to favour, but he never regained the manor of Chatham. In 1289, Chatham was granted to Guido Ferre for the period of his lifetime. The manor continued to be passed on through various noble families throughout the Middle Ages. Poll tax records from 1377 show that Chatham had around 300 inhabitants, half of whom were employed on the river or on ships. The majority of them probably lived in cottages near the parish church of St Mary and others in a settlement along the river.

By the 1480s Chatham had developed into a small fishing and agricultural village, bordered to the north by the great walled city of Rochester and to the east by the Half Hundred of Gillingham. The great maritime discoveries of the period were opening the world to seagoing trade and exploration. King Henry VII deeply involved himself with the encouragement of international commerce by financing the fitting-out of ships and expeditions to unknown regions. Although these merchant vessels were armed they were manned by privateers. At this time England possessed no navy and relied upon hiring these armed merchantmen to protect their shores in wartime. Henry realised that this was a situation fraught with danger and began ordering the laying down of keels for the creation of a Royal Navy. The earliest vessels were built at Deptford on the Thames, but there is some conjecture that one of these ships may have been constructed at Chatham. The National Maritime Museum has in its collection a painting of a vessel, *The Great Harry*, which it states was built at Chatham Dockyard in 1488. However, there was certainly no royal dockyard at Chatham at that time, although there may have been some shipbuilding yards; but whether any of them would have been capable of building such a large warship is of some doubt.

When Henry VIII came to the throne in 1509 he continued to build a strong navy. The major Royal Dockyard in the earlier years of his reign was at Portsmouth, where ships such as the *Mary Rose* were built. In later years Portsmouth's importance declined in favour of the three Thames-side yards – Woolwich, Deptford and Erith. However, all four of these dockyards had some major disadvantages. Portsmouth was vulnerable to attack from French ships in the Channel while the Thames yards were a long way upstream and the larger ships based there would take days to negotiate the narrow passage of the river's shallower waters to make their way to the open sea at times of emergency. Subsequently, as the number of ships in Henry's navy grew, the need for a new anchorage near to the Thames became a priority and the naval authorities decided upon a stretch of the River Medway then known as Gillingham Waters (now better known as Gillingham Reach) for such an anchorage.

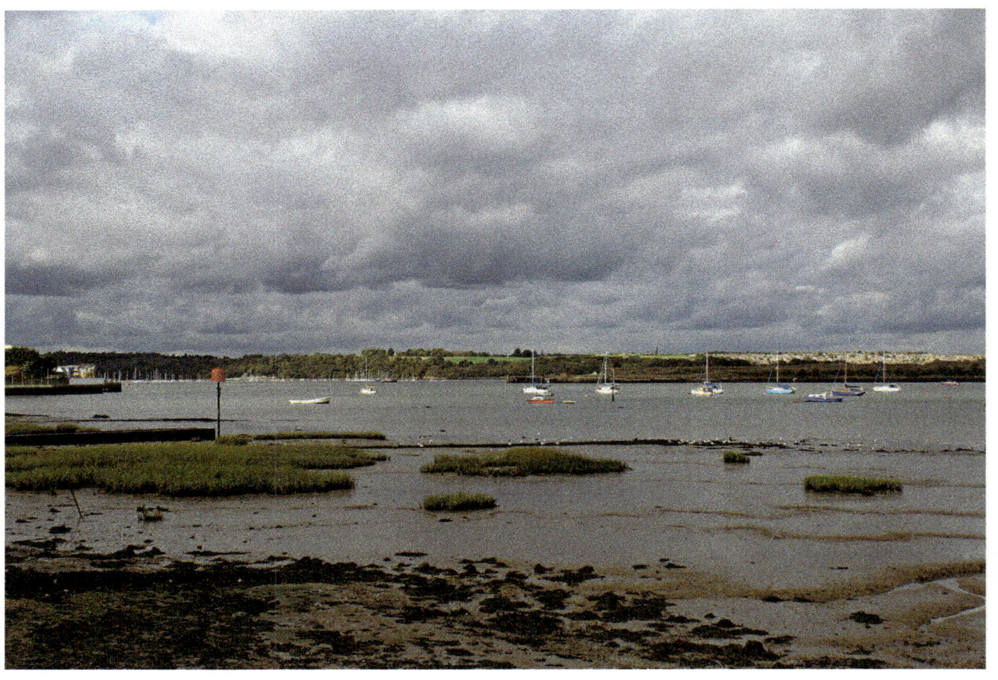

Gillingham Reach.

The location offered several advantages: the waters were slow running and there was a good rise and fall of tide. The surrounding hills provided shelter from strong winds and winter storms and there were plenty of sites along the riverside mudbanks where vessels could be 'grounded' to expose their undersides for maintenance and cleaning. Within a few years the Medway became a safe, regular winter anchorage for Henry's navy. In 1510, a dock was built at Chatham on a site around 100 yards south of St Mary's Church to aid with the maintenance of the ships.

In the annual accounts for 1547 rendered by the Treasurer of the Navy to the Exchequer a sum of £4,167 is recorded for expenditure on the ships anchored at Gillingham. Included in that figure was an item of thirteen shillings and sixpence as rental for a storehouse close to 'Jillyngham Water' for one year payable to a Thomas Wynnall. The precise location of this building is unclear, but it's possible it could have stood somewhere in the vicinity of what is now Gillingham Pier.

This storehouse would have been used to store ropes, masts and other equipment while the ships lay at anchor over the winter months. By 1561 further storehouses had been rented with the cost to the exchequer rising to sixty shillings and fivepence. By this time the navy's ships were now anchoring a little further upriver at Chatham Reach, so it's reasonable to presume that some of these later storehouses were located within Chatham itself. Indeed, recent archaeological digs have uncovered remains of a Tudor storehouse below St Mary's, Chatham's parish church, and it's this area of land between the church and the river where the first dock had been built in 1510 that was developed into the Elizabethan Chatham dockyard.

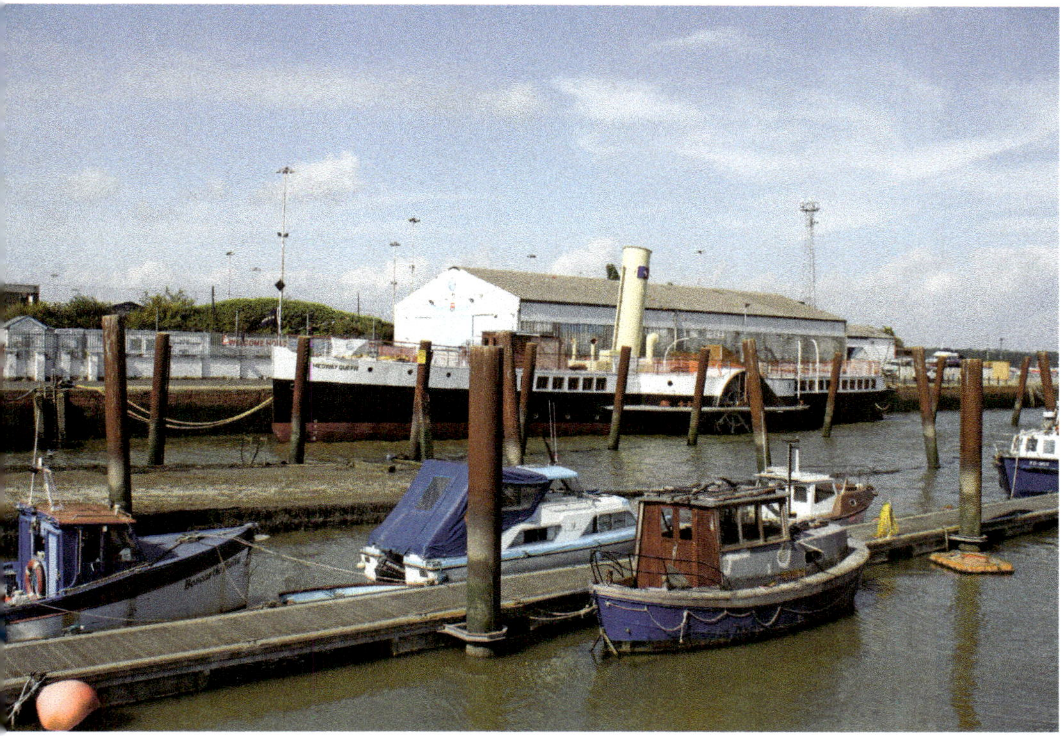

Gillingham Pier, the possible site of the first Medway naval storehouse.

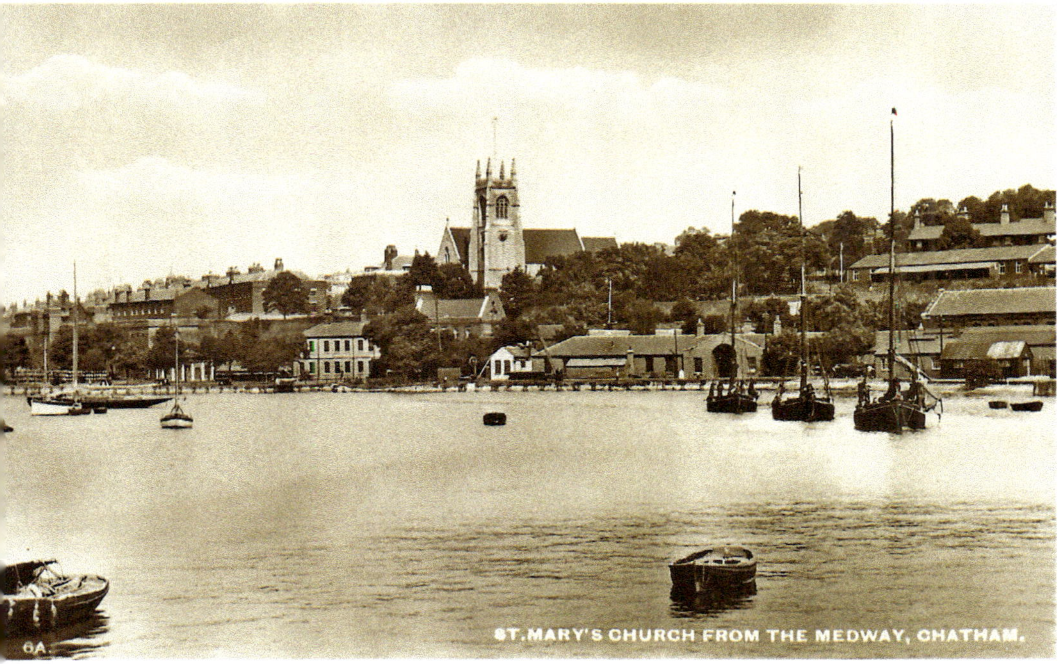

St Mary's Church and the site of the Elizabethan dockyard.

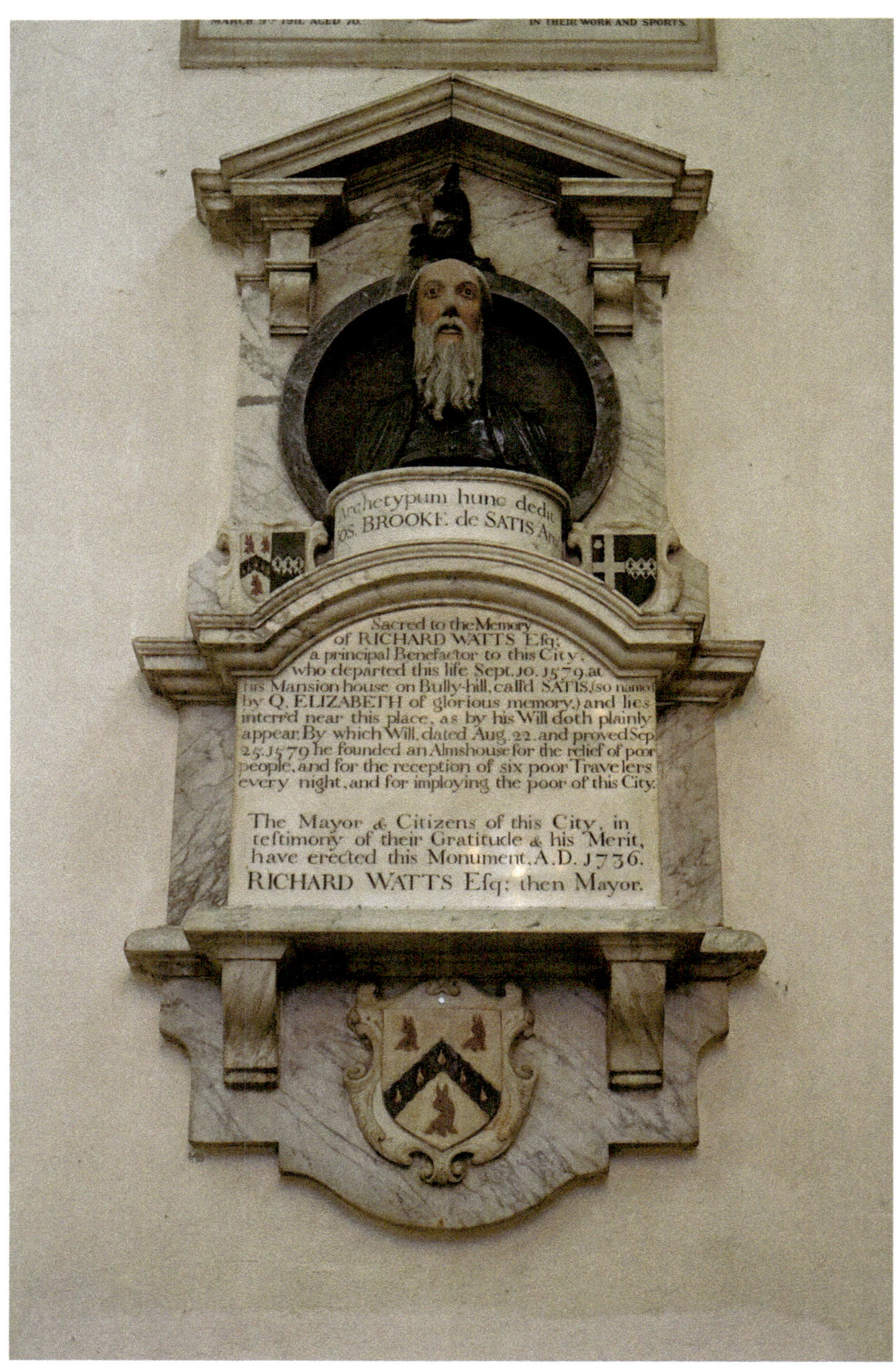

The memorial to Richard Watts in Rochester Cathedral.

As the ships moored on the Medway grew in number many the older vessels that had come to the end of their service life were converted into accommodation hulks to house the increasing numbers of shipwrights, sawyers, carpenters, riggers, sailmakers and other workers who had come to work on the fleet at Chatham, in some cases accompanied by their families.

The early years of the reign of Elizabeth I saw the Medway grow in importance to the navy, and in 1567 the Navy Board established its headquarters at Chatham. A victualling storehouse was purchased at Rochester to provide a supply of food and drink for the increasing number of ships moored in the river. Basic repair and maintenance facilities were built along the waterfront below the church and in 1570 the construction of a mast pond was completed. The mast pond enabled the mast timbers that had been cut from fir trees to be stored in the pond underwater to prevent them from drying out before being fitted to ships. Prior to storage in the pond the timbers would have been cut and formed by the mast-makers in a mast house. Hill House, a large property owned by the Dean and Chapter of Rochester, was leased to provide offices for the administration of the new yard and accommodation for its senior officers. Within a year further land had been rented and more storehouses and a forge constructed on the site. The year 1573 saw Queen Elizabeth visiting the Medway to review her fleet. She remained here for four days, staying at the Crown Inn at Rochester, but she also dined with Rochester MP Sir Richard Watts at his house on Boley Hill. Watts had been appointed Deputy Victualler of the Navy in 1554, a position that saw him based at Chatham. He had already accumulated substantial wealth as merchant supplying victuals to the ships based on the Medway from his storehouses at Rochester, so his official appointment to the navy was a logical step.

The year 1580 saw the construction of a major new wharf at the dockyard site, which was an extension of the one already existing on the site. The new wharf mounted a crane to offload a ship's guns and other heavy equipment before it went into the dock for repair or was laid up on the river for winter. In 1581, a new dry dock was completed. This new dock was used to grave the navy's various galleys (oared sailing ships). At first the entrance of the dock was sealed by a dam, but within a year the dam had been replaced with gates. The first galley to use the dock was the *Eleanor*, a large vessel captured from the French in the 1560s.

By the mid-1580s the dockyard was now officially known as 'Chatham Dockyard' and its importance to the nation's defence was soon to be proved.

2. The Spanish Armada and Wars with the Dutch

With the increasing concentration of the fleet on the River Medway in the sixteenth century, attention turned to the river's defences. Fear of a French invasion in 1539 had prompted Henry VIII to order the construction of new castles at Deal, Walmer and Sandown to protect the Kent coast, and blockhouses at Higham, Gravesend and Tilbury to defend the Thames Dockyards. These were all artillery fortifications designed for a new type of warfare with low walls that reduced their profiles and substantial earth ramparts to increase their strength and provide platforms for guns. The medieval Queenborough Castle on Sheppey was the only fortification that prevented an enemy fleet entering the Medway and that had fallen into some decay. Henry had ordered its repair in 1536 and by 1542 the repairs were complete. The castle was now an artillery fortress. At the same time, a new blockhouse was also constructed at Sheerness and in 1547 the treasury accounts tell us of the gunners' wages at both forts: 'eight persons serving in the Castell of Queensboroo and the Blockus at Shere Ness of thyle of Sheppey were paid ... after the rate of sixpence by the day every man'.

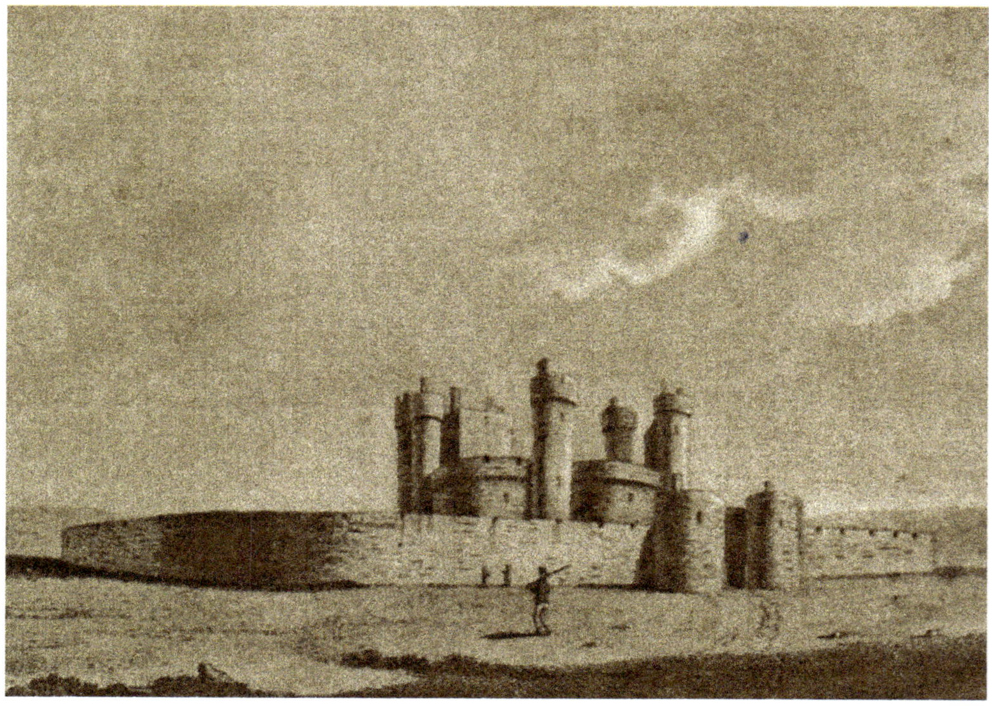

Queensborough Castle.

In 1559, a year after Queen Elizabeth's accession to the throne, she and her privy council ordered a bulwark (a form of artillery bastion) to be built at Upnor on the left bank of the Medway, opposite Gillingham. The site chosen to build the bulwark consisted of around 6 acres of land that belonged to Mr Thomas Devinisshe of Frindsbury. That same year the office of the Treasurer of Marine Causes was ordered to pay Devinisshe twenty-five pounds for the site. Upnor Castle, as it became known, was designed by Sir Richard Lee, Engineer of the Ordnance. He was assisted by Humphrey Locke, who was variously described as Overseer, Surveyor and Chief Carpenter. It was Locke who recommended the use of stone from the walls surrounding Rochester Castle. Other stone came from the ruins of Malling Abbey, which had been seized by Henry VIII in 1538 and then stripped and pillaged by locals.

The man chosen to be Paymaster and responsible for the day-to-day management of the project was Sir Richard Watts of Rochester (see chapter 1). By order of council all bulwarks of the realm came under the jurisdiction of the Lord High Admiral, and so this brought Upnor Castle under the control of his local representative, the Officer in Charge of Chatham Yard. By 1567 the castle was completed, and the original gun platforms extended and improved. The fixed establishment was set at one master gunner and seven gunners.

By the 1580s fear of invasion from France had been replaced by fear of invasion from Spain. The Medway was vulnerable to raids mounted from the Spanish-controlled ports in the Low Countries and when war eventually broke out with Spain in 1585, a chain was stretched across the river below Upnor Castle to St Mary's Creek. The chain was supported

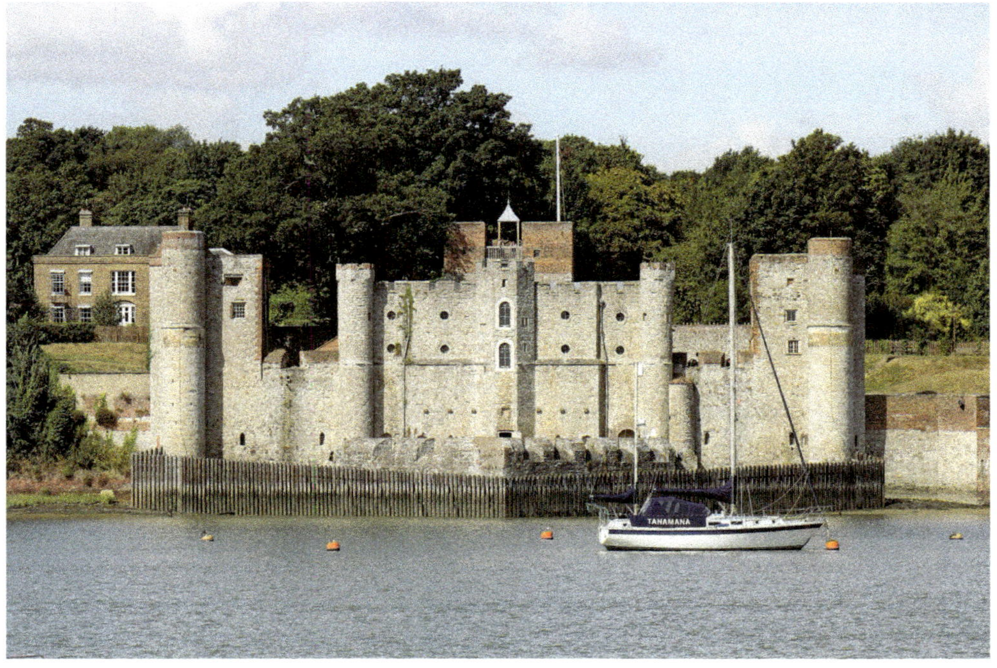

Upnor Castle.

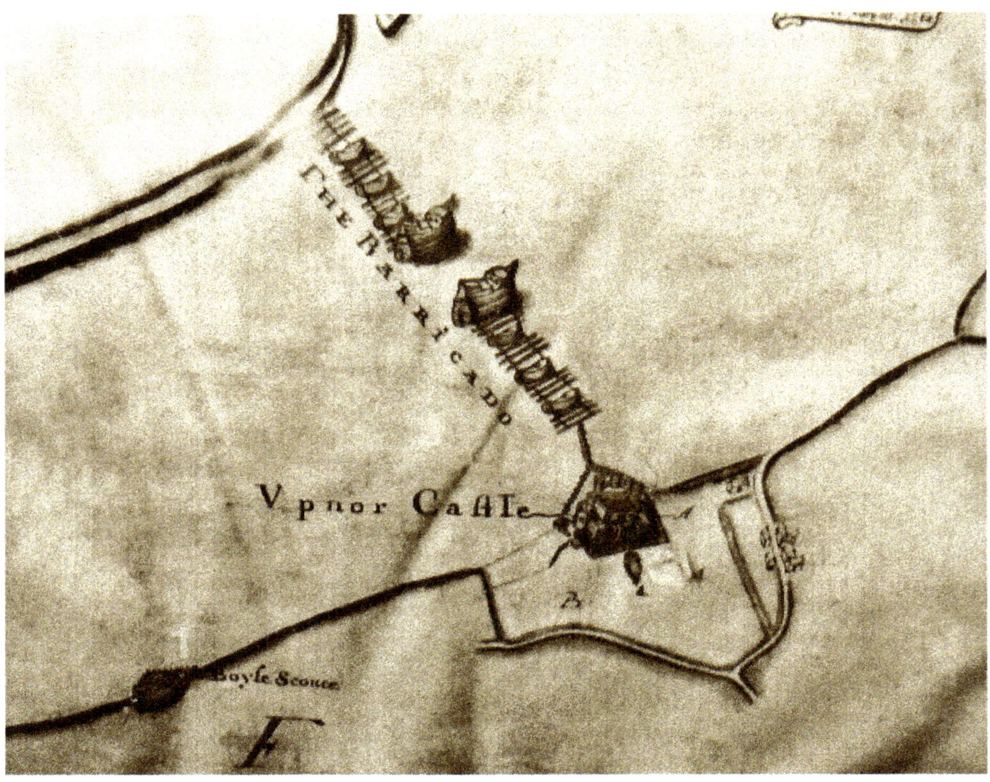

Seventeenth-century map showing the chain across the river below Upnor Castle.

by lighters and secured at one end to a set of piles on St Mary's Island. The chain was operated by two large wheels housed on a pier head at Upnor. The chain remained raised to prevent enemy shipping entering the river to attack the fleet assembled there. It could be lowered to the riverbed to allow the passage of friendly vessels attempting to make the journey upriver but only after they had been met, challenged and inspected by teams of armed seamen posted aboard naval pinnaces based on the river. In support of the chain defence a watchtower was built in the dockyard and a bell fitted to a nearby storehouse to sound the alarm if any enemy vessels were sighted attempting to enter the river. The chain was later moved further downriver between Hoo and Gillingham. The Medway's defences came under the direction of Sir John Hawkins, Treasurer of the Navy, who had been appointed to keep the navy in good repair and who later would become a major supporter of seamen's charities.

In December 1587, the English fleet was assembled at Chatham, where it was inspected by its Commander-in-Chief, Lord Howard of Effingham. One of the vessels was a pinnace, the *Sunne,* the first ship built at Chatham Dockyard. Most of the other ships present had been maintained and made ready by the dockyard. Lord Howard could find no signs of neglect or bad workmanship on any of the vessels and passed them as all being of the highest quality. The fleet left the Medway in April 1588 and headed west to Plymouth to rendezvous with a smaller fleet under the command of Sir Francis Drake.

On the night of Friday 29 July 1588, the emergency beacons all along the south coast were lit to flare out the warning that a large fleet of Spanish ships had been spotted in the Channel. A total of 130 vessels carrying over 10,000 soldiers and 2,600 artillery pieces were making their way to invade England. On Sunday 31 July the Armada, as it came to be known, headed for Calais and it was here and at other points along the Channel over the following few days that they were confronted by the English fleet and their fireships, which had been lying at anchor in Portsmouth. The English sailing ships, much smaller in size compared to the Spanish oared galleys, were heavily outnumbered. However, their greater speed and manoeuvrability enabled them to get among their enemy, wreaking death and destruction as they went and managing to evade the Spanish grappling irons.

Chatham's contribution to the defeat of the Armada cannot be denied. As previously mentioned, most of the English vessels had been maintained at the dockyard. Many of the vessels, although built in Thames shipyards, had been designed by two of Chatham's Master Shipwrights: Peter Pett and Matthew Baker. Another point of note is that the English Commander Sir Francis Drake had spent his childhood at Chatham, where he fell under the influence of the many seamen he met and who no doubt encouraged his future career.

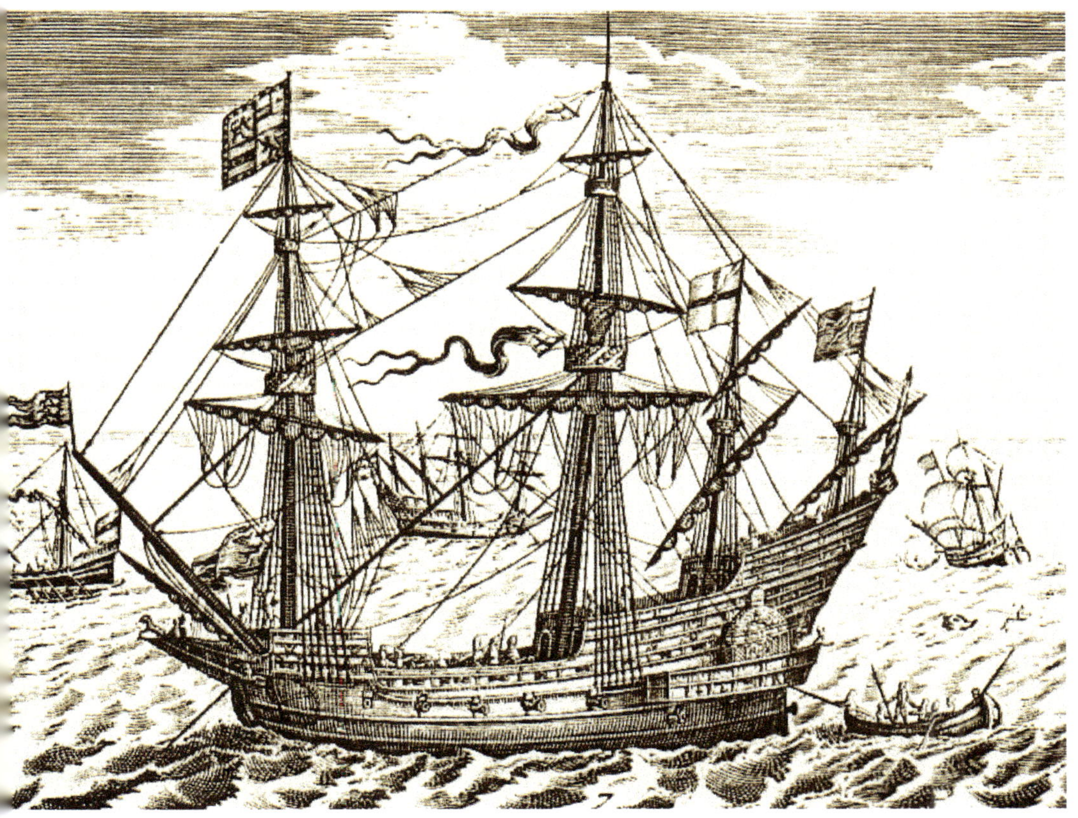

A ship of the Elizabethan Royal Navy.

The death of Queen Elizabeth in 1603 brought to an end to the house of Tudor. She was succeeded by James I, a Scot who had little appreciation of the English Navy and who considered it a drain on the nation's finances. Despite the king's indifference, the dockyard at Chatham continued to expand. In 1604, a new wharf was built to the north of the yard adding over 3,800 square feet to its area. However, the site of the yard with the presence of the church, a mill and numerous private dwellings around it ruled out any further expansion. In 1618, such was the growing importance of Chatham the decision was made to move the dockyard to a much larger site downstream. This was a decision that would have been made years earlier but for King James' reluctance to approve the expenditure. In 1619, 80 acres of land was leased for the construction of the new yard, which was to be supervised by Phineas Pett, son of the earlier Master Shipwright Peter. The new dockyard soon began to take shape: a dry dock was completed by the end of 1619 together with wharves and cranes. Three ranges of buildings, forming three sides of a rectangle, were built consisting of officers' houses, entrance gates, a sail loft and storehouses. The area enclosed by the ranges housed the dry docks, workshops and timber stores. Beyond this enclosure, to the south, a ropeyard and stables were added.

The new dockyard continued to rely upon Upnor Castle for its main defence. The castle had undergone a programme of repair and enlargement between 1599 and 1601. Repairs were made to the gatehouse and drawbridge; the height of the bastion was raised and a new gun platform and stone parapet added to it. A large wooden palisade was built in

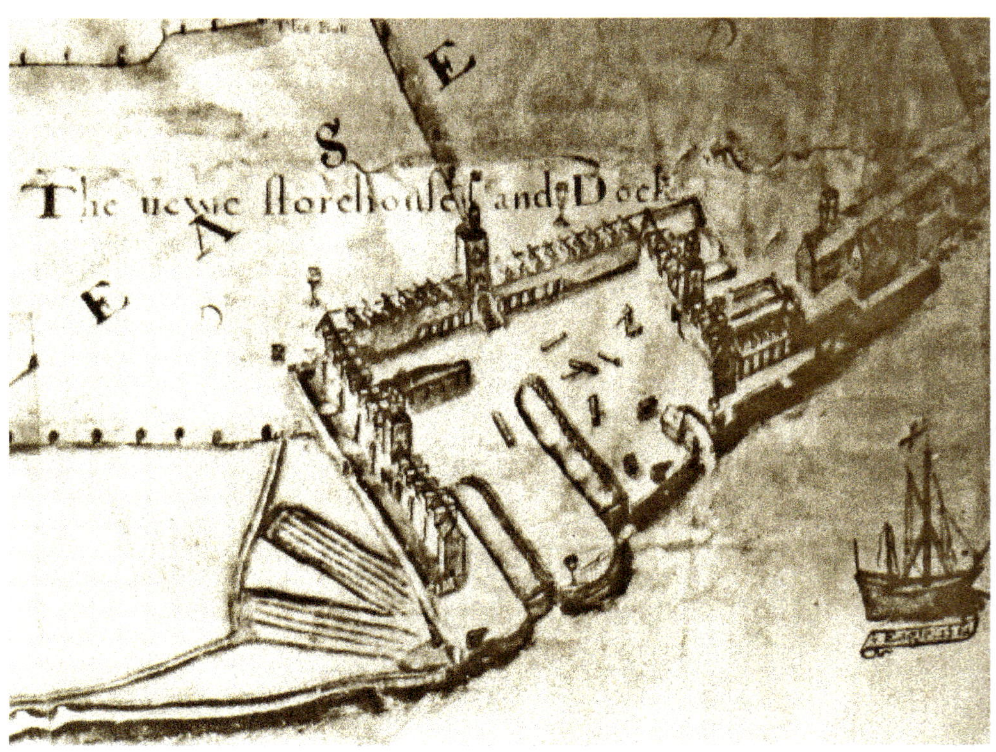

Seventeenth-century map showing the new Stuart dockyard.

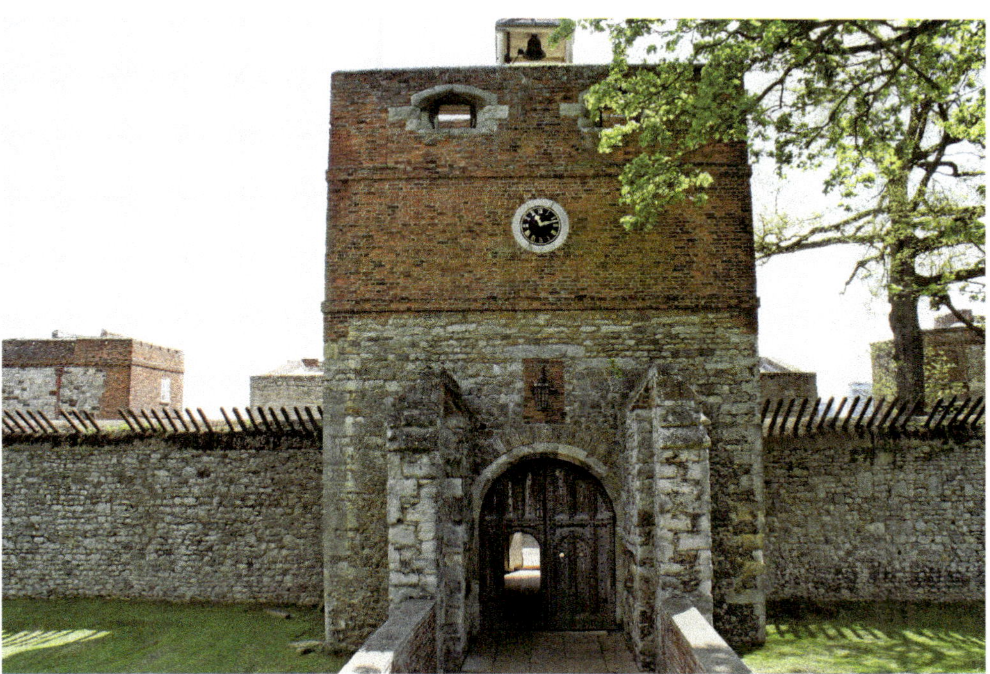

The Gatehouse at Upnor Castle.

front of the bastion. Further repairs had to be made to the gatehouse in 1653 following a severe fire that destroyed five rooms.

During the English Civil War (1642–51) Chatham's sympathies lay with Cromwell's Parliamentarians while neighbouring Rochester remained loyal to the King. The castles at Rochester and Upnor were occupied without a fight by the Parliamentarian forces and the dockyard was willingly placed into their hands by its commissioner, Phineas Pett.

Following Cromwell's victory in the Civil War, the new Commonwealth administration sought to mend relations with Holland, which had been strained during the war due to the Dutch support for the Royalist cause. In 1651, Cromwell sent a delegation to The Hague with the suggestion that the Dutch ally themselves to the Commonwealth to assist the English fight against Spain. This proposal was rebuffed, and the English envoys found themselves violently harassed by mobs until they left the country. This reaction prompted Cromwell to seek confrontation with the Dutch. His administration passed the Navigation Act requiring all goods imported into England to be carried either in English ships or vessels from the exporting country. This meant that Dutch ships could no longer carry goods from North America to England. When he came to power Cromwell had initiated an ambitious programme of naval expansion. Many new ships were added to the fleet, some of them built at Chatham, so the navy was in a strong position to engage the Dutch. The two countries inevitably drifted into a war, which raged for two years, during which the dockyard at Chatham undertook the bulk of repair and maintenance of the ships engaged in the North Sea and the Channel. A peace treaty was eventually signed in 1654; however, the treaty left the contentious issue of trade unresolved and with it the seeds of future confrontations were sown.

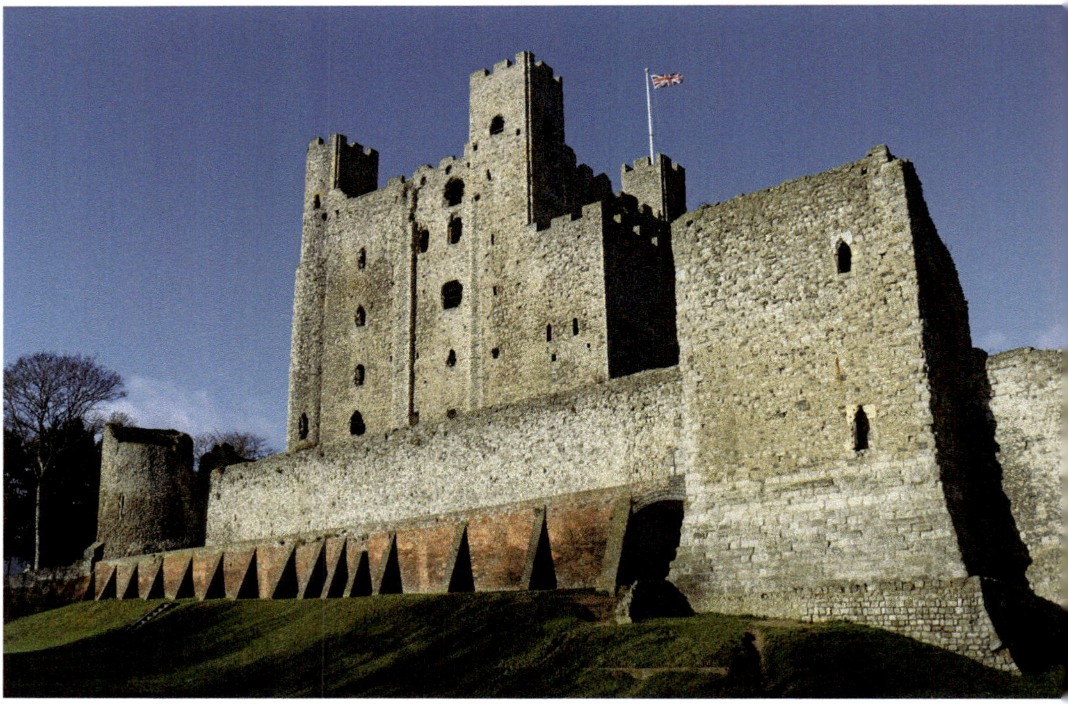

Rochester Castle.

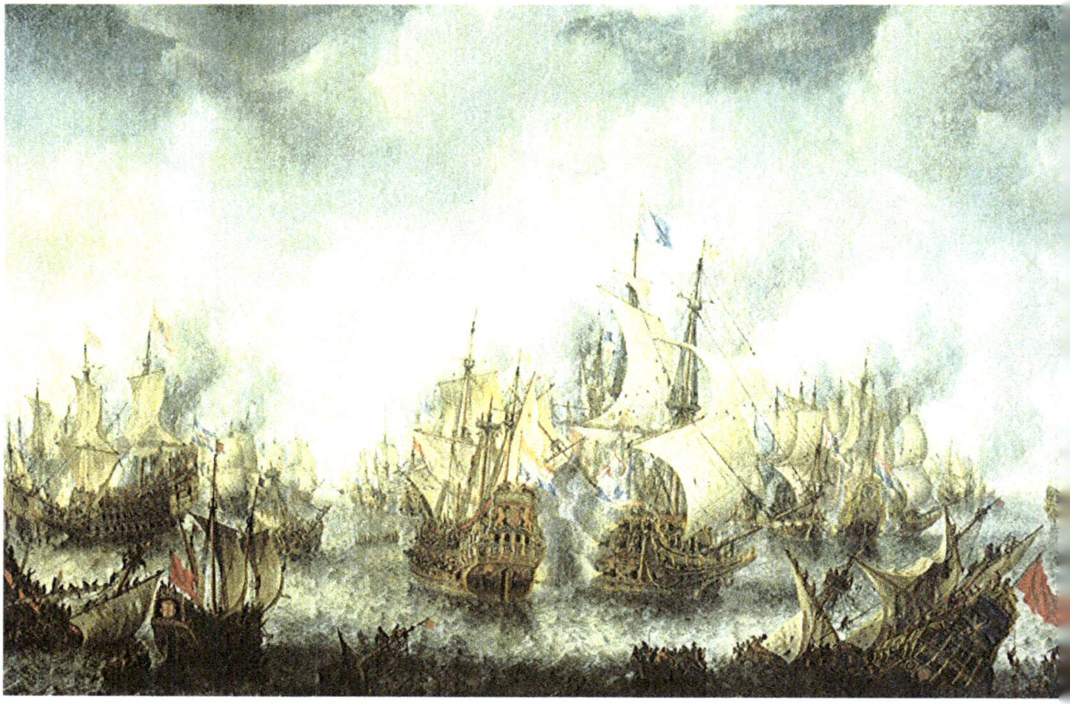

The fleets clash in the final battle of the first Anglo-Dutch War.

In May 1660 the Commonwealth administration came to an end and the monarchy was restored in the body of Charles II. On 29 May, the eve of his Restoration, Charles stayed the night at Rochester and the following day the king inspected his ships at Chatham. Charles took a keen interest in the navy and appointed his brother, the Duke of York (later King James II), as Lord High Admiral.

The King sought to remain on friendly terms with the Dutch in recognition of the support they had shown him during his exile from England. However, in 1664 the Duke of York persuaded Charles that renewing the war with the Dutch could bring substantial benefits to England, particularly by seizing the Dutch colonial possessions in North America, the Caribbean and Africa. On 24 June, the English invaded the Dutch North American colony of New Netherland and had control of it by October. The Dutch responded by attacking English trading posts in West Africa. On 13 June 1665, the two

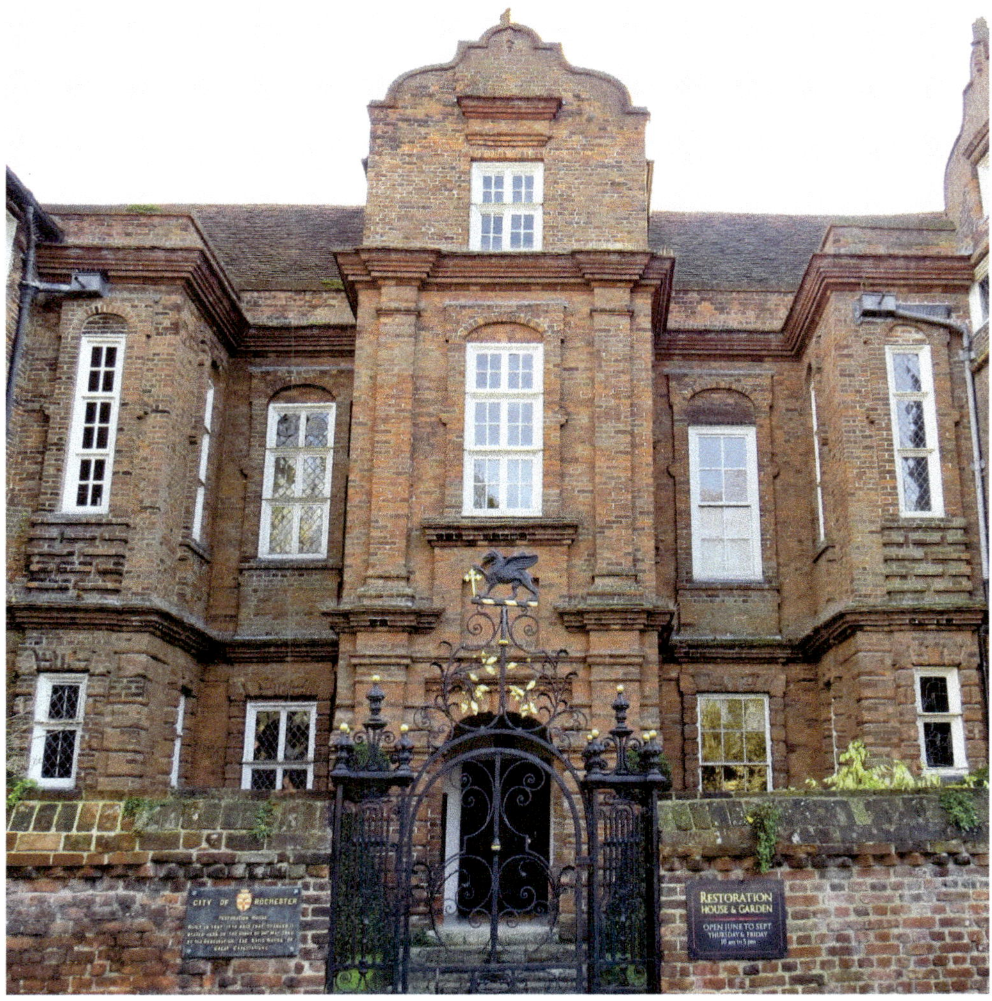

Restoration House, Rochester, where Charles II stayed on 29 May 1660.

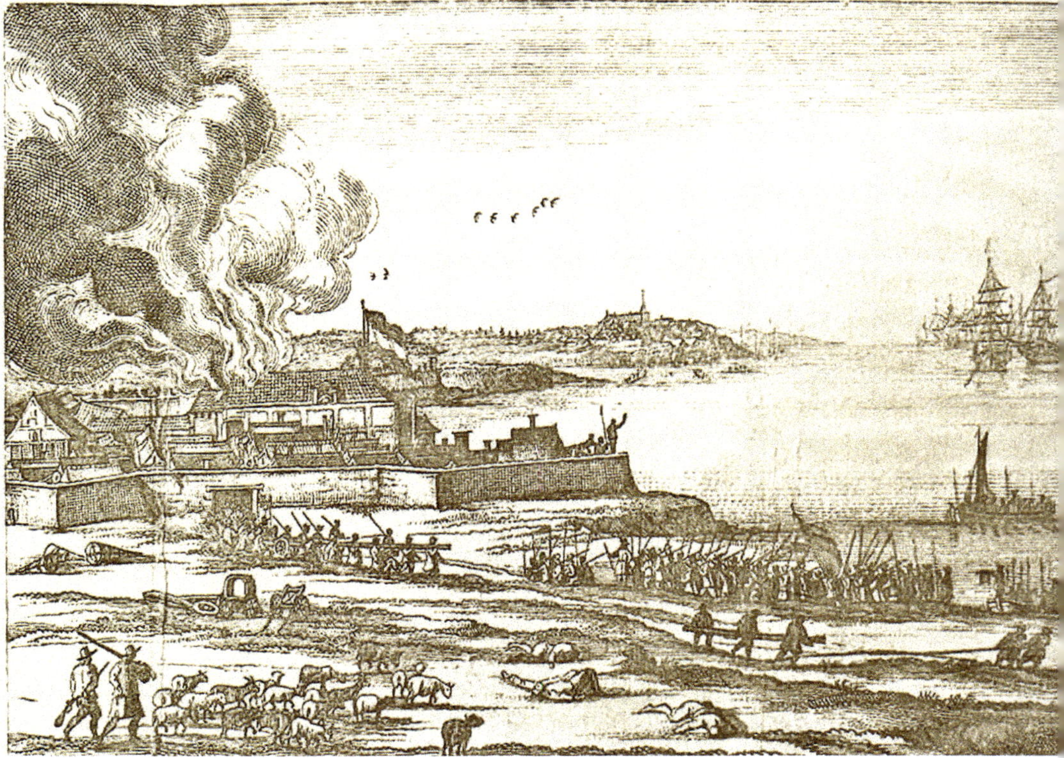

Contemporary Dutch print of the raid on Sheerness.

opposing navies clashed in the North Sea at the Battle of Lowestoft. The English won a major victory and further naval successes the following year persuaded the English government that there was little more to fear from the Dutch Navy. In 1667, it was decided that economies could safely be made by withdrawing the English fleet to its home bases and relying on fortifications for the nation's defence. This complacency was severely punished when, on Monday 10 June 1667, a squadron of the Dutch fleet under the command of Vice Admiral Willem van Ghent appeared in the Thames Estuary. The squadron attacked and ransacked Canvey Island and then proceeded to Sheerness, where they lay siege to the small fort there which was then still under construction.

Despite being rapidly reinforced from the garrison at Sittingbourne, the constant withering fire from the Dutch ships and the hindrance of the incomplete fortifications forced the defenders to abandon the fort. After landing troops to occupy the Sheerness fort, van Ghent's squadron rejoined the main Dutch fleet under the command of Admiral Michiel de Ruyter, who had already decided that his next move would be to sail into the Medway and strike against Chatham.

When news of the attack on Sheerness reached Chatham, panic set in. Ships that should have been moved to safer anchorages were left on the wrong side of the chain downriver at Gillingham. Many vessels were left unarmed and to compound an already dangerous

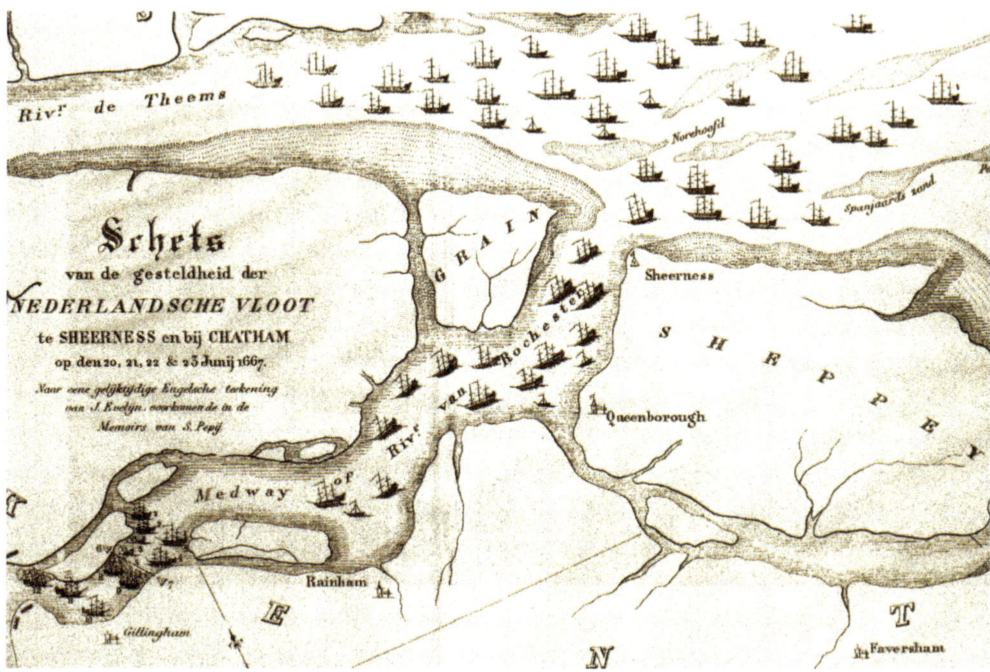

Contemporary print of the progression of the Dutch fleet along the Medway.

situation, Dockyard Commissioner Peter Pett appeared to take leave of his senses. Instead of using every available man to defend the yard, he used many of them to carry away his personal possessions, including his valuable collection of ships models. In the meantime, he ordered several good ships to be sunk in the river in a vain attempt to prevent the Dutch reaching Upnor.

On Tuesday 11 June, the Duke of Albemarle arrived at Chatham to take charge of the defences. Although he found over 800 men in the dockyard, they were so gripped with fear as to be almost useless as defenders. He also discovered that most of the yard's boats had been taken by other yard workers who had fled upriver to escape from the Dutch. The duke quickly tried to restore some order to the chaos: he set up two-gun batteries each end of the defensive chain at Hoo and Gillingham and ordered three ships to be positioned close to the chain to prevent any Dutch attempt to lower or break it.

On the morning of 12 June, van Ghent's squadron entered the Medway, arriving in sight of the chain and the three ships defending it. The one vessel forward of the chain was the *Unity*; she was attacked by the Dutch and successfully boarded. At some point during the engagement the chain was broken, and van Ghent sent fireships through it, targeting the other two English guard ships: the *Mathias* and the *Charles V*. Both vessels were soon ablaze and the way was clear for van Ghent to continue on to Chatham. Unbelievably, when his squadron arrived along the river just below Upnor Castle they found the English flagship, the *Royal Charles*, at anchor and unguarded. Van Ghent sent out a boarding party of just nine men who captured the ship without a shot being fired.

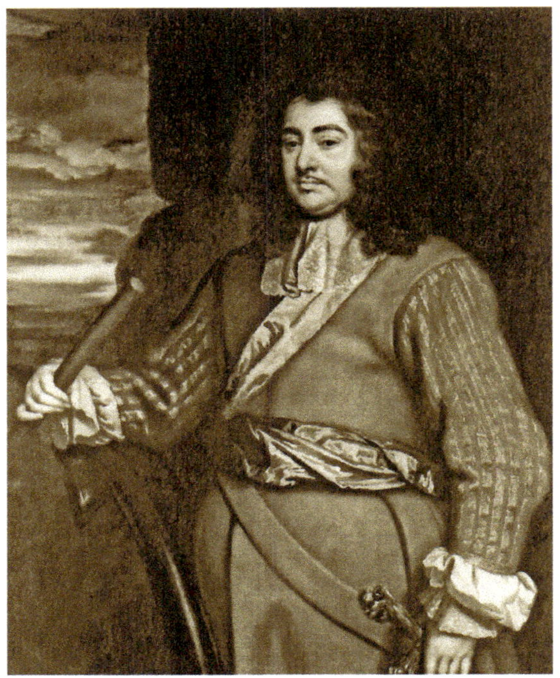

Left: George Monck, 1st Duke of Albemarle.

Below: The stern carving of the *Royal Charles* now on display in Amsterdam Museum.

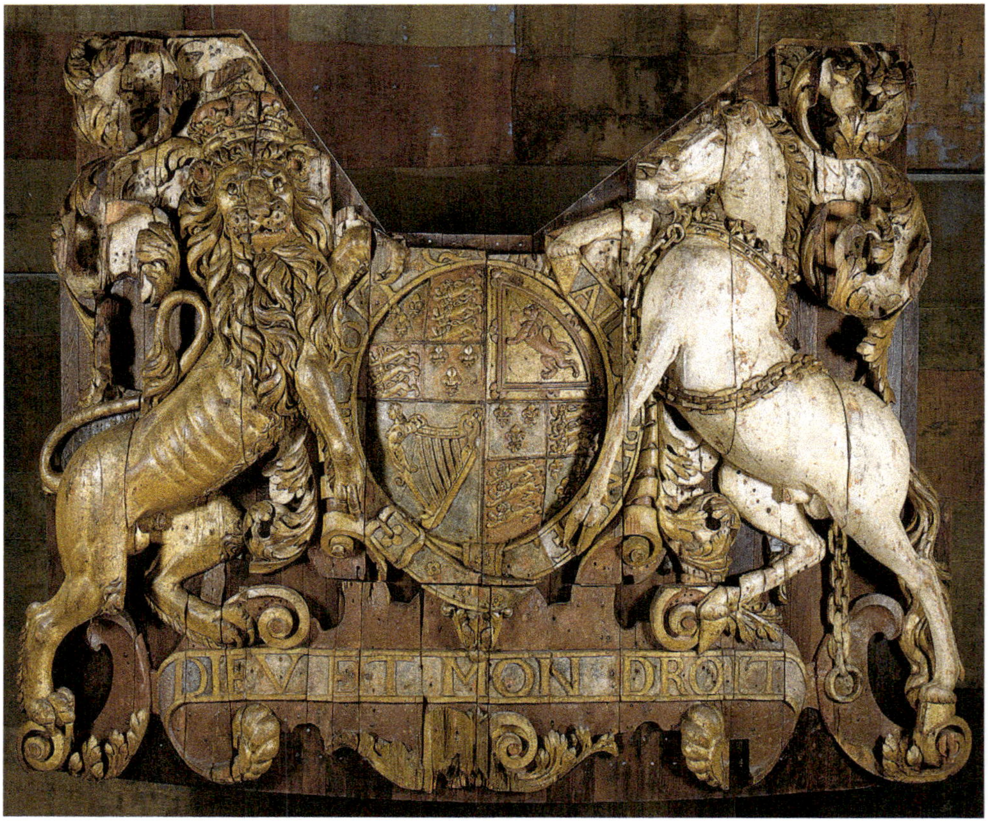

When the tide turned the Dutch anchored for the night ready to resume operations in the morning. In the meantime, Albemarle reinforced the defences at Upnor Castle with a hastily constructed eight-gun battery beside the castle. On Thursday morning, van Ghent sent his remaining five fireships upriver with an escort of warships. Three more English ships were destroyed, but the Dutch had come under very severe fire from the heavy guns of the new battery at Upnor Castle, convincing van Ghent to halt the attack and withdraw downriver to Queenborough where it rendezvoused with the rest of the Dutch fleet and presented its commander, de Ruyter, with the prize of the *Royal Charles* now sailing under a Dutch flag.

When news of the attack on Chatham and the humiliating loss of the *Royal Charles* became known, anger swept the nation. On 16 June, a warrant was issued for the arrest of Dockyard Commissioner Peter Pett, who was consigned to the Tower of London charged with several seditious practices and misdemeanours. The most serious of these charges was that he had ignored orders given as far back as March to move the *Royal Charles* upriver to a safer anchorage and then on 11 June, the day after the Dutch attack on Sheerness, he had refused Albemarle's order to move the vessel. Pett was eventually released from the Tower on bail in December 1667 and dismissed from office in February 1668. The lessons learnt from the only serious assault ever to be undertaken on the dockyard would change the face of Chatham forever.

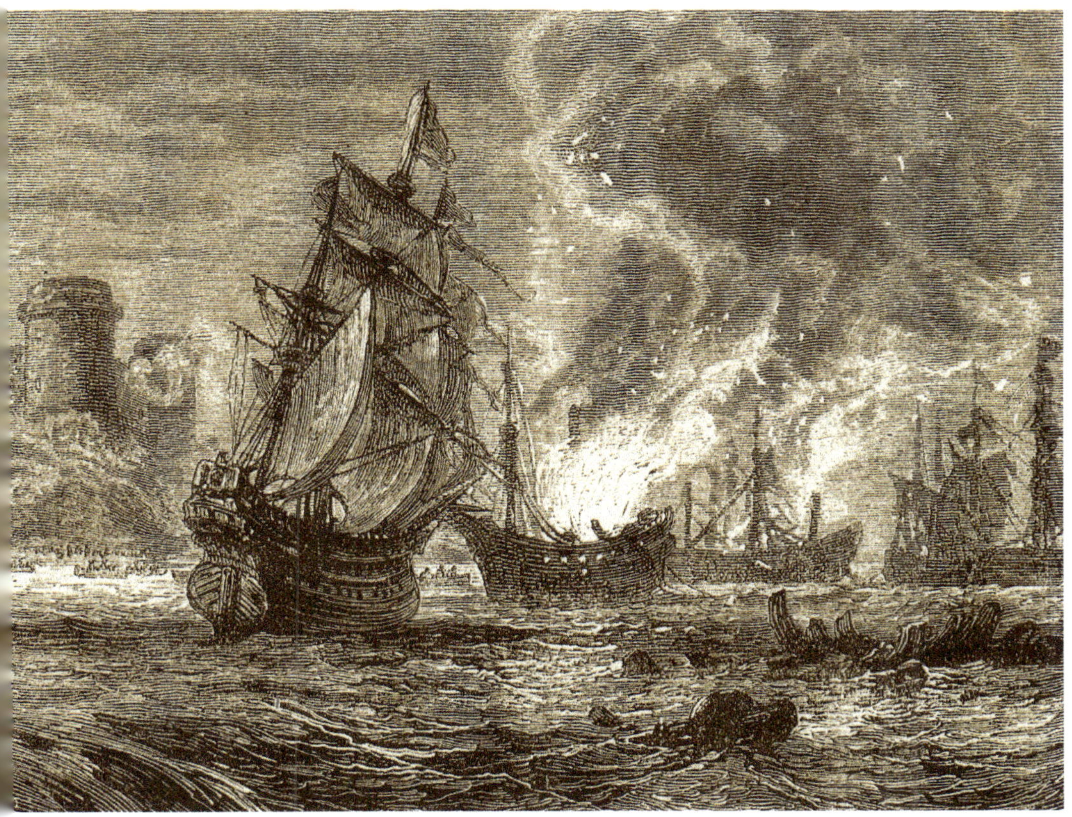

The Dutch fleet under fire from Upnor Castle.

3. Wars with France

Following the Dutch raid on the Medway and the signing of the ensuing peace treaty, a revision was made of Chatham's defences. There were obvious deficiencies that had to be quickly made good and the king's cousin, Prince Rupert, now the navy's senior admiral, was ordered to the Medway to direct the operations. All ships were now ordered to be moored upstream from Upnor Castle and new gun batteries constructed north of the dockyard. A new boom was placed across the river at Gillingham and a stronger garrison of over a thousand men was based at Strood, Rochester and Chatham. Longer-term plans were also made for building two new forts along the river at Gillingham on the dockyard side and Cockham Wood on the Upnor side.

The forts were designed by Chief Engineer Sir Bernard de Gomme and were under construction by 1669. When completed the two new forts would provide devastating crossing-fire against any enemy ships that managed to breach the new chain across the river. Other gun batteries were built on islands in the Medway at Hoo Ness, Bishop's Ness and Oakham Ness. A consequence of the revised defence plans was that Upnor Castle was now redundant as a fort and in 1668 it was ordered to be converted into a powder magazine and weapons store. By 1691 the castle held 5,206 barrels of gunpowder – more even than the Tower of London, which was only holding 3,692 barrels.

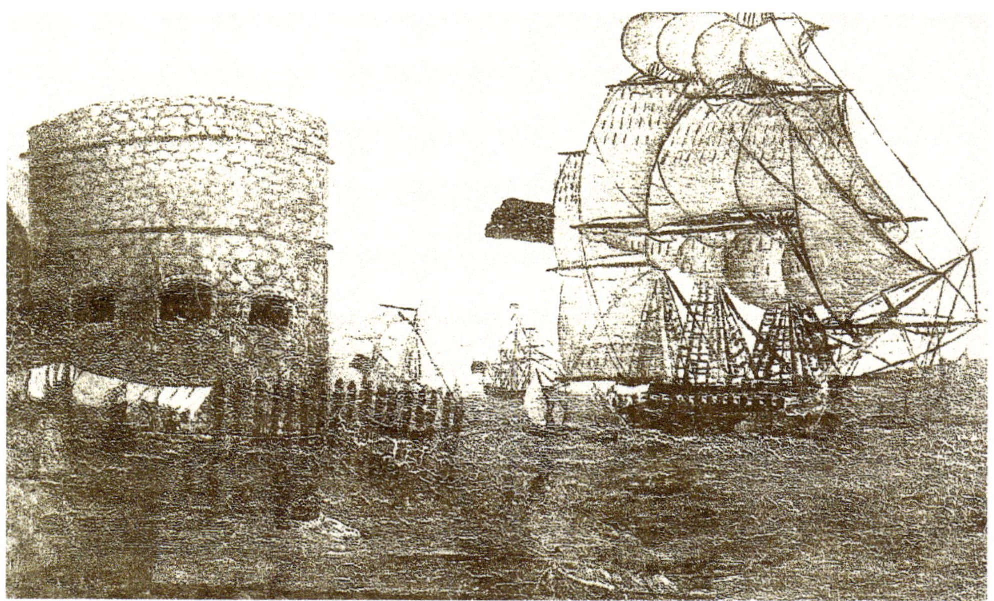

Gillingham Fort.

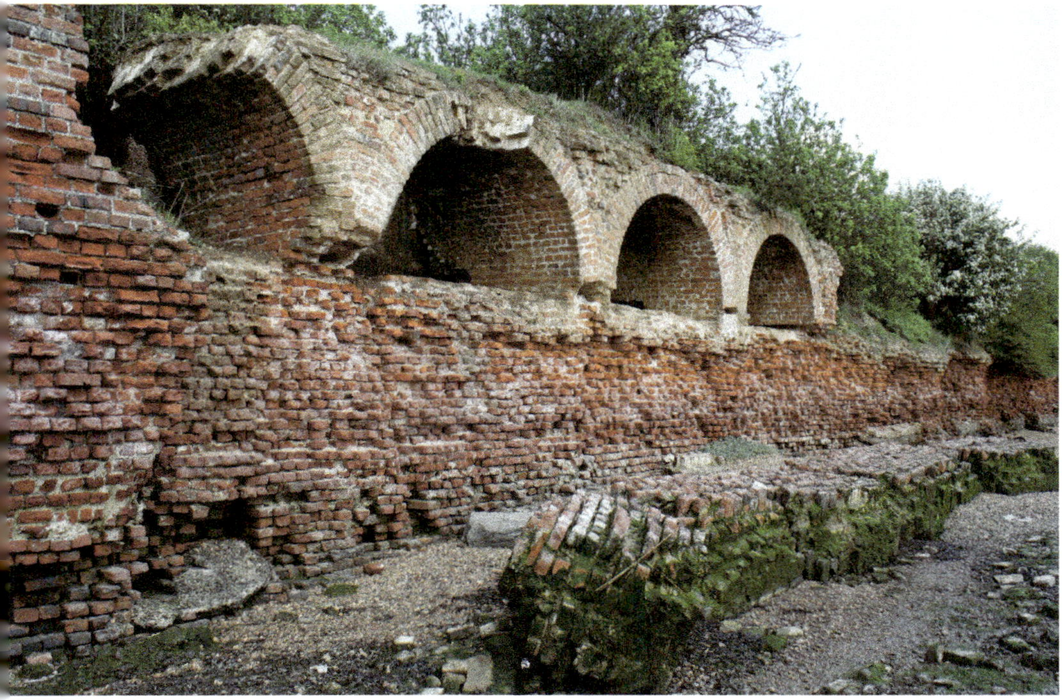

The remains of Cockham Wood Fort in 2012.

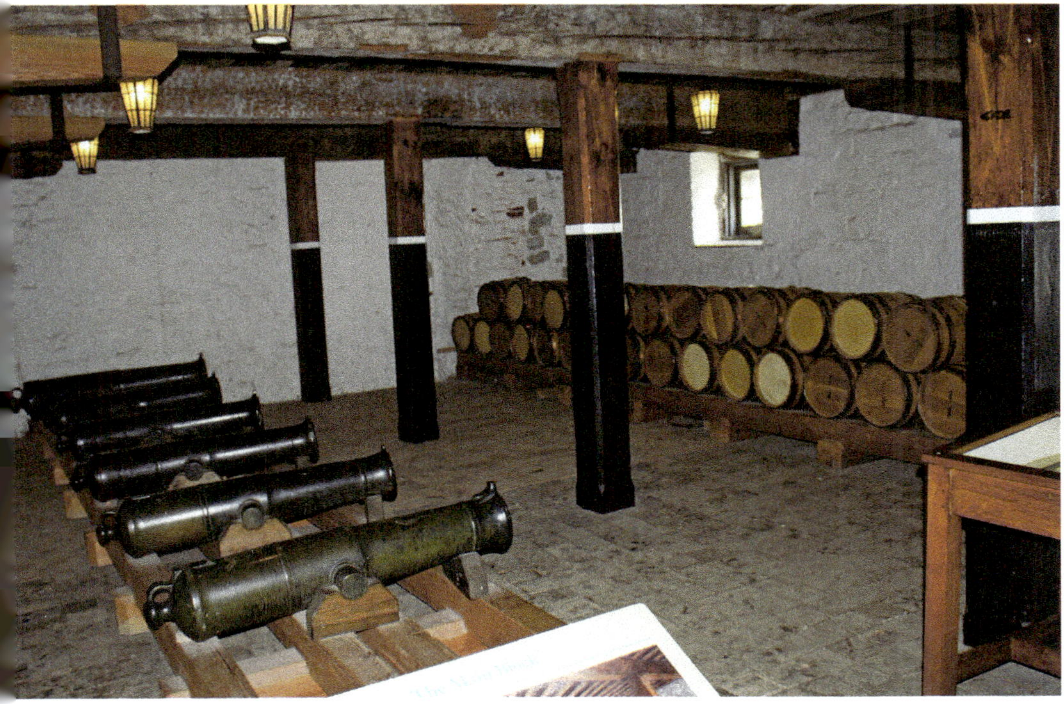

Ground-floor powder magazine at Upnor Castle.

The 'Glorious Revolution' of 1688 saw the Catholic King James II deposed and replaced by his Protestant daughter, Mary, and her husband, William of Orange. James was exiled to France along with many of his Jacobite supporters. The French regarded James and his heirs as the only legitimate ruling dynasty and were keen supporters of plans for a Jacobite invasion of England to restore James to the throne. As a prelude to this invasion, in 1689 James landed in Ireland with an army of 6,000 French troops and linked up with his Catholic supporters there. However, the campaign was a failure culminating with James' defeat at the Battle of the Boyne in 1690. Despite James' defeat, conflict with the French continued for a further seven years and reached several parts of the globe. English sea power was an important factor in their eventual victory. By the end of the war the French could only muster 137 warships against England's 323, many of which had been built at Chatham.

The Act of Union of 1707 saw the kingdoms of England and Scotland united under one throne and guaranteed the Protestant succession which, once again, stirred up Jacobite and French resentment. Britain and France were already on opposing sides in the War of the Spanish Succession and in 1708, with fears of a French invasion in the air, John Churchill, the 1st Duke of Marlborough, who was then Master General of the Ordnance, asked Queen Anne to authorise various new defensive works at strategic points around the country including a fortification at Chatham on the high ground behind the dockyard. Proposals were submitted by Royal Engineer Talbot Edwards for a series of linear fortifications supplemented with bastions on the high ground east of the dockyard. A Government Commission of Inquiry was held at the Rochester Guildhall to consider what land and houses would need to be purchased for the Crown

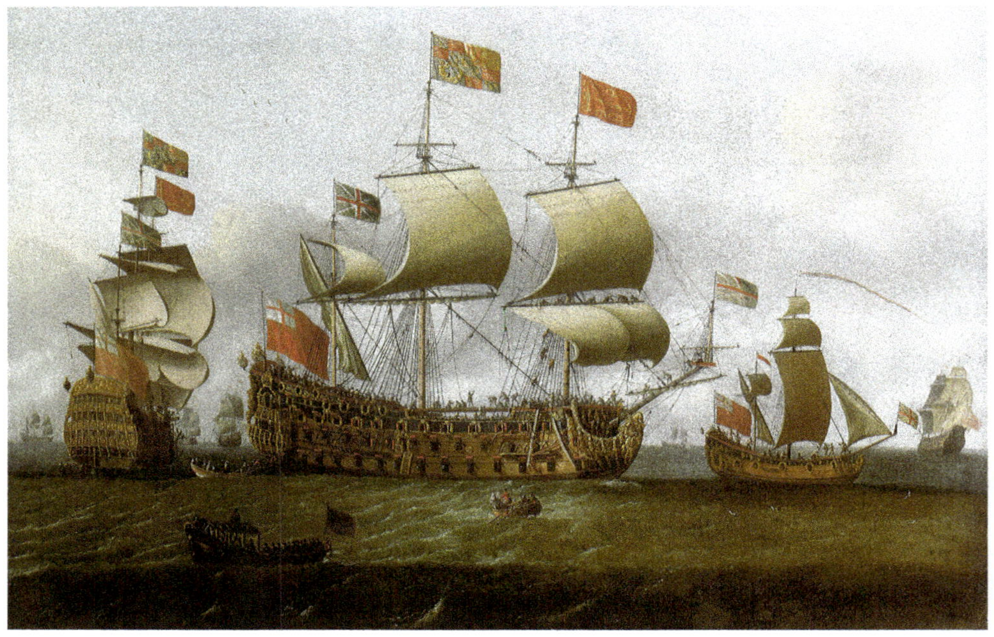

HMS *Britannia,* a Chatham-built first-rate launched in 1682.

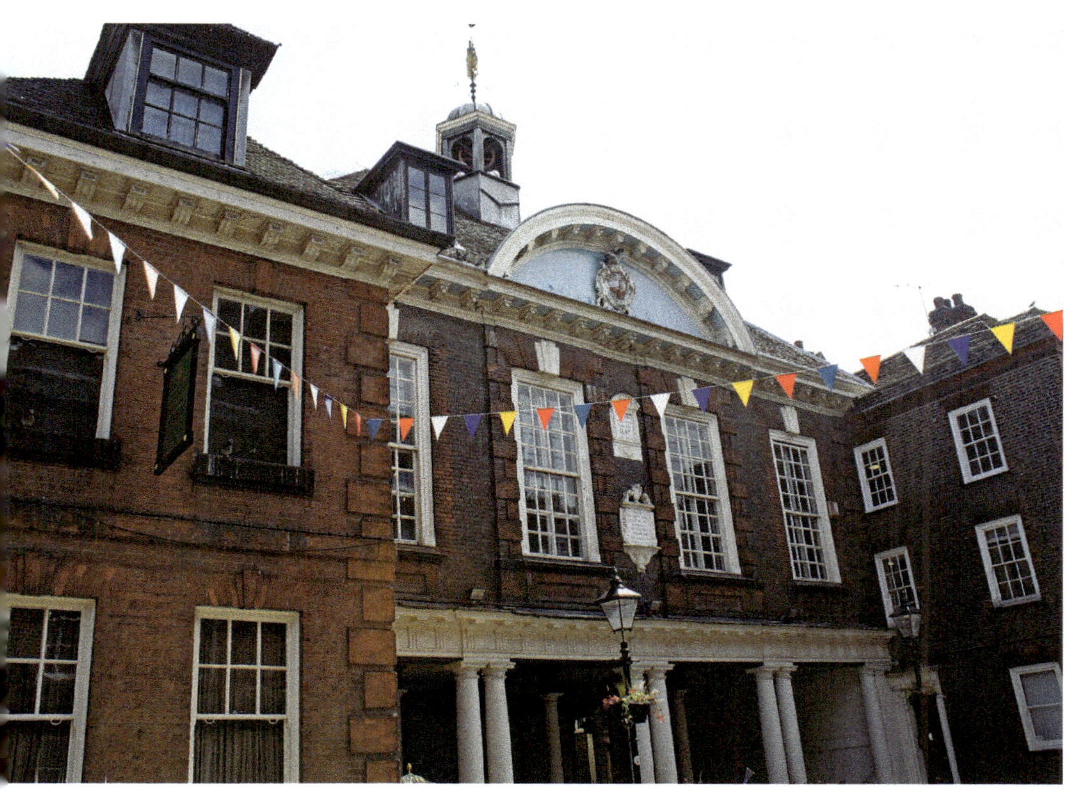

Rochester Guildhall.

to construct the new defences. An Act of Parliament in 1710 authorised the purchase of the land, but the Continental war was proving a drain on Britain's finances, so the necessary financial transactions were not completed, and the new defences remained, for the time being, unbuilt.

The Peace of Utrecht was signed in 1713, bringing the War of the Spanish Succession to an end. But with the death of Queen Anne in 1714 and the succession of the Hanoverian George I to the throne, Jacobite resentment resurfaced yet again. France broke the peace treaty by refusing to recognise the new British king and threw its support behind the Jacobites, renewing fears in Britain of a French invasion. Those fears led to a new Act of Parliament, which once again authorised the purchase of the land necessary for the construction of Chatham's new fortifications. This time the transactions were completed, and the land acquired for the Crown at a cost of £16,734. The fortifications however remained, for the time, unbuilt and the lands leased, first to the Queen's Serjeant-at-Arms Charles Goatley and then, in 1725, to Sir Edmund Bacon of Gillingham.

During this period, the dockyard continued to grow in importance. The Commissioner's House, a grand residence befitting the dockyard's most senior officer, was built in 1703. Between 1718 and 1722 new boundary wall and crenelated gatehouse were built to surround the land perimeter of the yard, which had expanded northwards to allow for the construction of new mast ponds and docks.

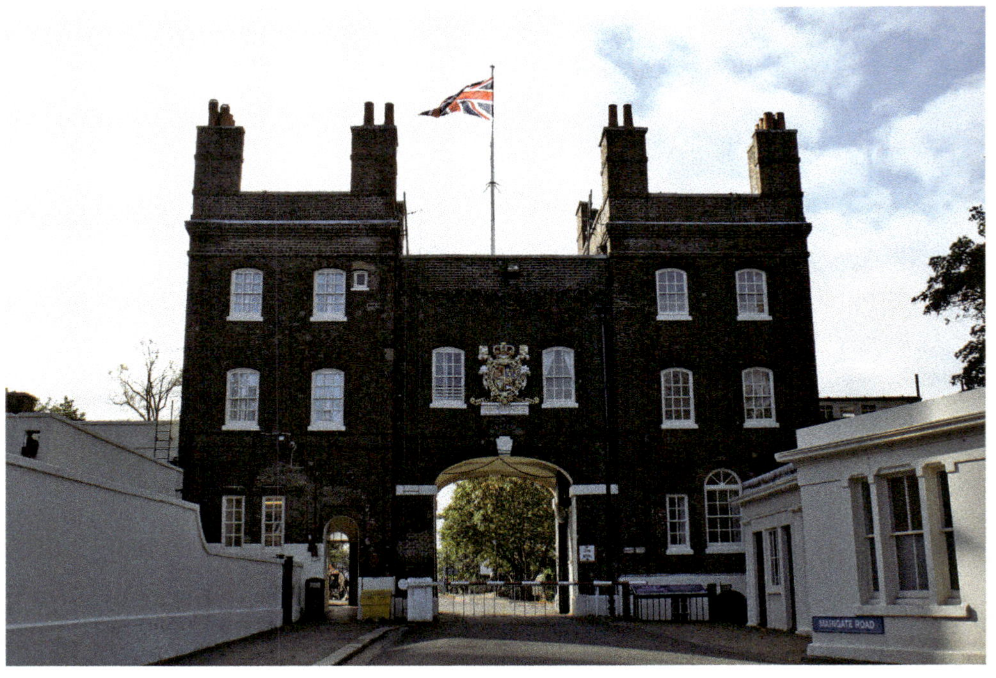

Main Gatehouse, Chatham Dockyard, built in 1722.

New storehouses and sail loft followed, and the Officers' Terrace was constructed between 1722 and 1731 as residences for the yard's other senior officers. The growing dockyard increased the demand for labour and so to accommodate the influx of workers and their families, a new settlement at Brompton was established around 1710. Meanwhile the old Tudor dockyard to the south had been taken over by the Board of Ordnance, who were responsible for the supply of arms, munitions and other battle equipment to both the army and the navy. The site was converted into a gun wharf where guns and ordnance could be unloaded and stored ready for use on warships. By the early decades of the eighteenth century the Gun Wharf was well established with three large storehouses, including the majestic-looking Grand Storehouse, built in 1705, and the Storekeeper's House, built in 1719.

The Board of Ordnance were also now responsible for the powder magazine at Upnor Castle and their concern about its security prompted the construction of a barracks to the south-west of the castle. Completed in 1719, it housed two officers and sixty-four men and was the first purpose-built barracks in the Chatham area.

The mid-eighteenth century saw yet more conflicts with France. First was the War of the Austrian Succession (1740–48), closely followed by the Seven Years' War (1755–63). Both wars saw the Royal Navy in action across the world and by 1756 Chatham Dockyard was employing more than 1,700 workers and was the largest civilian employer in the south-east of England, reflecting its importance as a naval base. The year 1759 saw what was to become one of the most momentous events in the dockyard's history, with the laying of the keel of Nelson's future flagship HMS *Victory*. The vessel was launched with great fanfare in 1765. The ceremony was attended by many dignitaries including the Lord Privy Seal William Pitt (who was later to become the 1st Earl of Chatham) and other ministers.

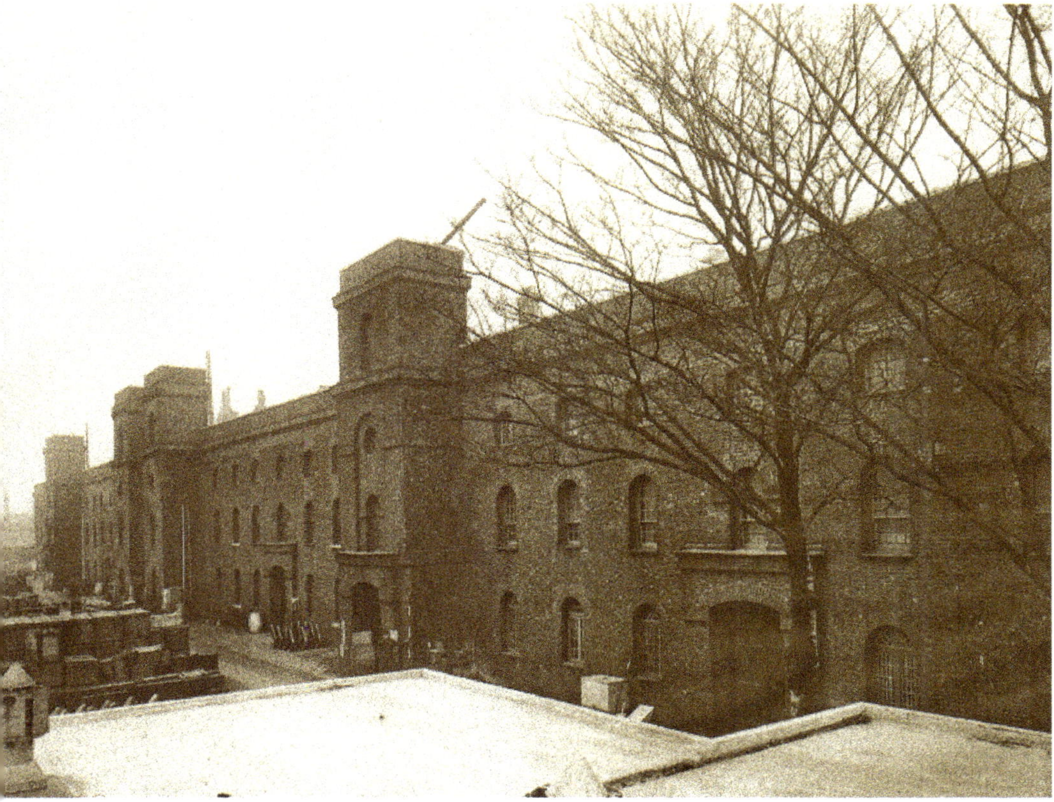

The Grand Storehouse at the Gun Wharf, built 1705.

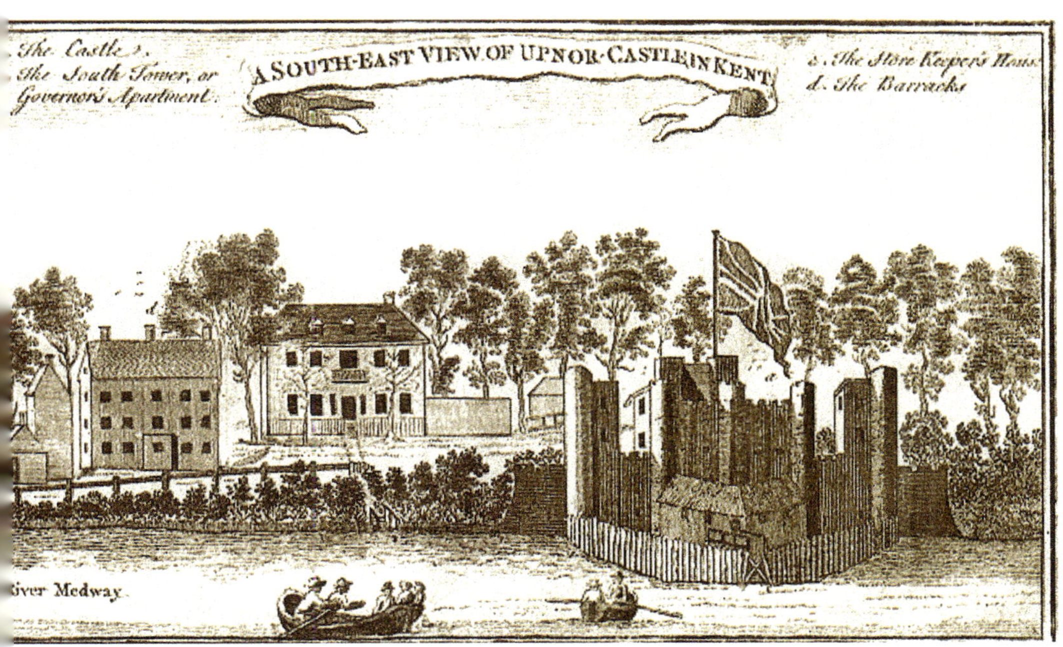

Eighteenth-century print of Upnor Castle with the barracks on the left.

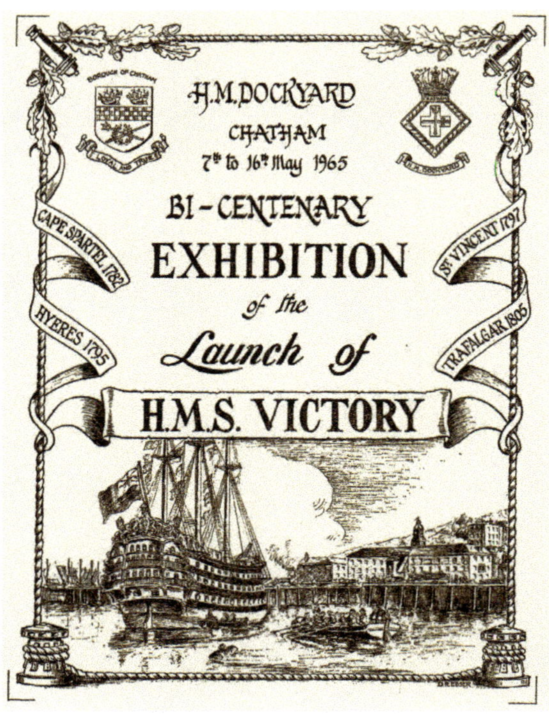

1965 exhibition programme celebrating the bicentennial of the launch of HMS *Victory*.

As always it seemed fears surfaced about a French invasion and the defences of the dockyard at Chatham were being questioned. By this period the defences at Gillingham Fort, Upnor Castle, Cockham Wood Fort and Hoo Ness Fort had fallen into neglect. Many of their guns had either been removed or were in a state of disrepair. In 1755, work at long last commenced to remedy Chatham's defensive shortcomings and create the new lines of fortifications that had first been proposed almost fifty years before.

Royal Engineer Captain Peter Desmaretz was appointed as superintendent for the construction of the new fortifications, which became known as the Chatham Lines. The National Archives holds a copy of Desmaretz's original orders stating:

> ...That Captain Desmaretz be appointed Superintendent of the Works at Chatham. That he be acquainted therewith and that he be directed immediately to make a demand of such entrenching tools and materials as shall be necessary to carry on the said Works...; That ... the following Engineers who are not employed at present, viz: Mr. Thomas Wilkinson, Mr. Hugh Debbieg, Mr. Robert Clerk, Mr. Richard Dudgeon and Mr. Manson be directed to attend Captain Desmaretz and to observe and to follow such orders as they shall from time to time receive from him...

Desmaretz provided the drawings and cost estimates for the works with Hugh Debbieg taking direct control of the construction. The first stage of construction was completed by 1757 and consisted primarily of earthwork defences in the form of ditches, ramparts and bastions. The Lines ran from the corner of the dockyard wall near St Mary's Creek in the

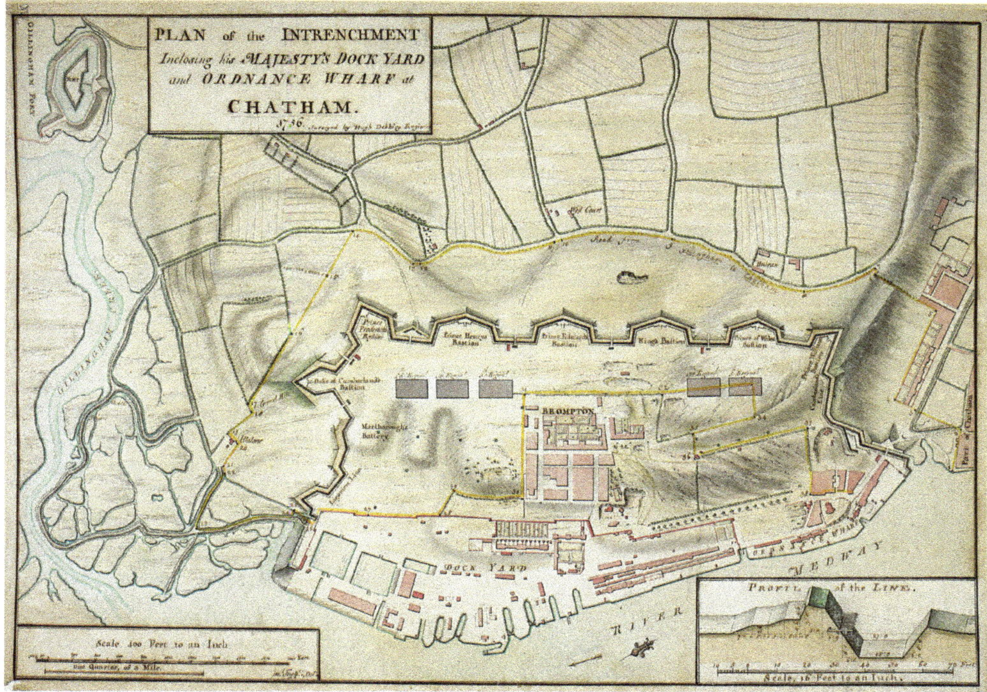

1756 map of Chatham Dockyard and the Lines.

north to the Gun Wharf in the south. Four great bastions provided the main features of the central section and were named, running north to south, Prince Henry's Bastion, Prince Edward's Bastion, King's Bastion and Prince of Wales Bastion. These bastions formed the main eastern defence. The northern defences consisted of a further two bastions, Prince Frederick's Bastion and Duke of Cumberland's Bastion, while the southern end was defended by Prince William's Bastion and the Cumberland Lines. At the Gun Wharf a wet ditch connected these southern defences to the river.

To man the new defences would require a garrison of over 1,800 troops. It was impractical to house this number of men in billets, as had traditionally been the case, so in 1758 Desmaretz submitted an estimate to the Board of Ordnance for the building of a barracks within the Lines capable of housing two battalions of 900 men plus their officers and a company of artillery. The site finally chosen for the new barracks was an area of land near the Gun Wharf between what is now known as Amherst Hill and Dock Road. The barracks were completed by 1763 and became known as Chatham Barracks.

A Royal Marine Division had been established at Chatham since 1755. When not serving on ships the marines were billeted with local households and inns, but by the 1770s increasing numbers made it necessary for some permanent accommodation to be found for them. In 1777, a site between the Gun Wharf and the dockyard was chosen for the construction of a new barracks, which were completed in 1779 and could house over a thousand men.

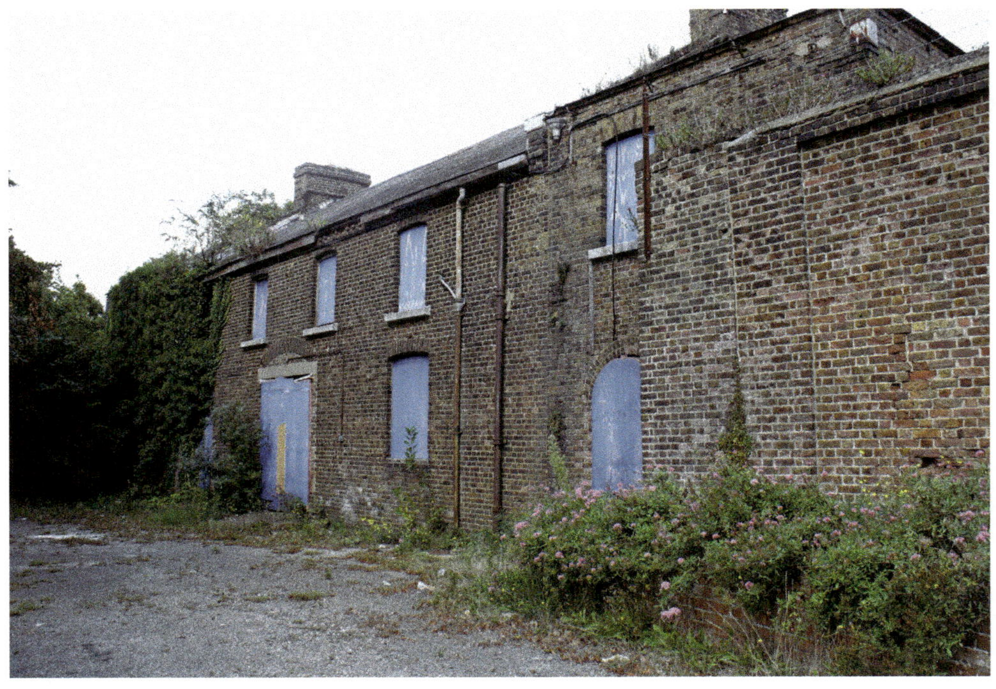

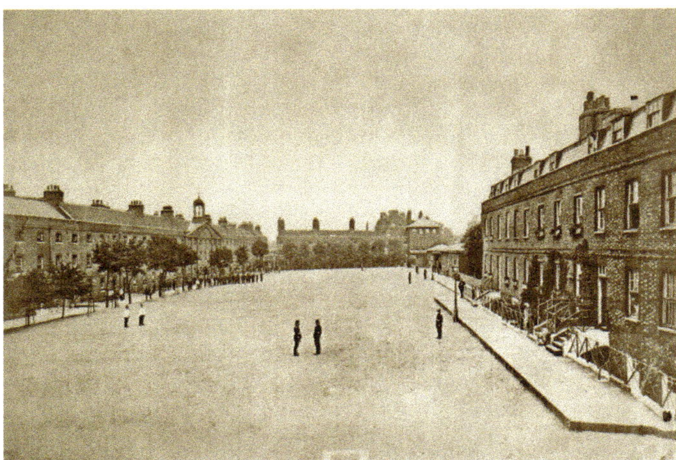

Above: The Ordnance Store at Chatham (Kitchener) Barracks, built 1795, awaiting redevelopment in 2014.

Left: The Royal Marines Barracks, built 1779.

The year 1779 also saw renewed threats of invasion from France. In 1775, the French had thrown their support behind Britain's American colonies rebelling against the Crown, and by 1778 France itself had waged war on Britain once again. In December 1779, royal consent was given to strengthening the Chatham Lines. Debbieg was again involved in designing the fortifications, which included new works to the north of the dockyard, a new redoubt and a new fort to dominate the high ground to the south. A couvre-port or defended gateway was also built on the Inner Lines to enable access to the field of fire between King's Bastion and Prince of Wales Bastion.

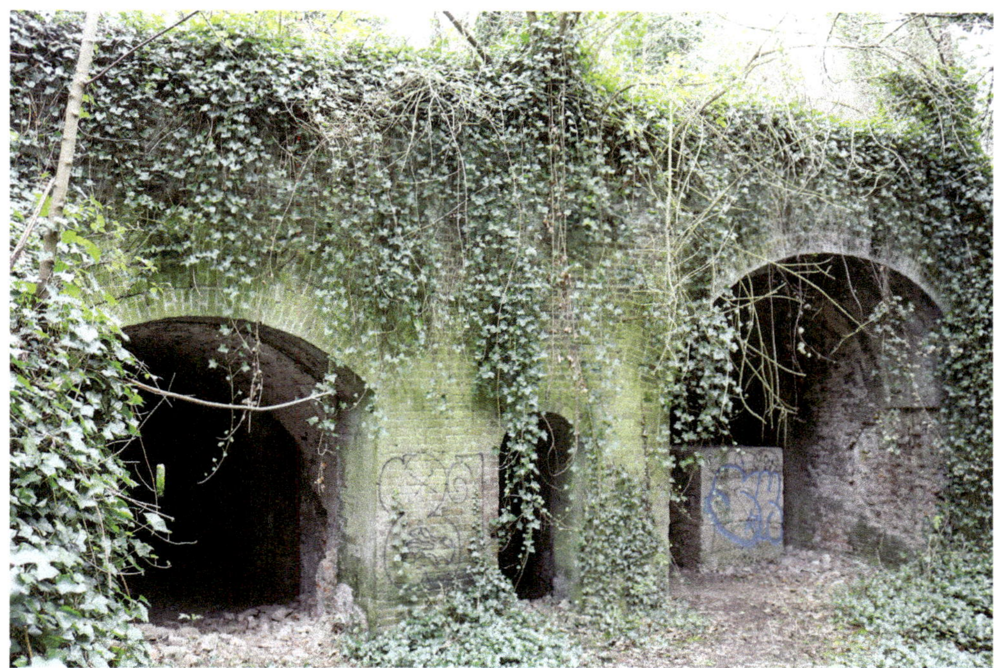

The Couvre-Porte (defended gateway) on the Inner Lines.

Despite the end of the American war and conflict with the French, by 1786 Townsend Redoubt had been completed in the north and Amherst Redoubt completed in the south. The latter, with its numerous associated gun batteries, tunnel network and fortified barracks, would become known as Fort Amherst. However little else of Debbieg's extravagant plans were allowed to come to fruition, much to his displeasure.

In the late eighteenth century, the French Revolution and subsequent rise to power of Napoleon Bonaparte saw Britain yet again under threat from across the Channel, with war between the two old foes breaking out in 1793. However, it was not until 1803 that work recommenced on strengthening Chatham's defences. The improvements to the Lines included the brick revetment of all the ditches and ramparts, the completion of the Lower Lines extending the defences to St Mary's Creek in the north and various works at Fort Amherst including construction of a new Barrier Ditch running down to the Gun Wharf, which had also been extended to handle the extra guns and munitions the new fortifications would require.

Consideration was also given to the lack of fortification on the high ground south of Chatham town and in 1805 Fort Pitt was built on a hill, which gave commanding views of the Lines, the dockyard and the River Medway. The approaches from Rochester Bridge were defended by Fort Pitt's two outlying gun towers: Delce Tower and Gibraltar Tower. A new military road was constructed in 1804 to connect Fort Pitt with the Lines just below Fort Amherst. The road was guarded at each end with a defended gatehouse. Fort Pitt's use as a defensive site was short-lived and by 1814 it was being used as a military hospital.

Further improvements were made to the southern defences when, in 1808, another new network of gun towers and ditches were built stretching from the River Medway to the

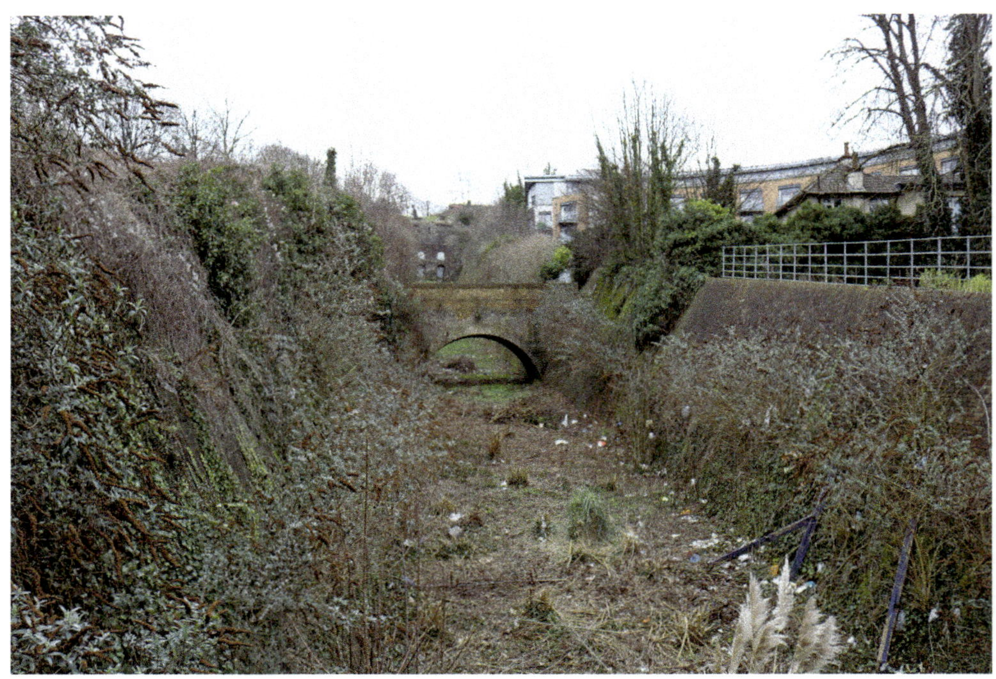

The Barrier Ditch looking up to Fort Amherst.

Rochester Maidstone Road to prevent an attacking force advancing from the Maidstone direction and seizing Rochester Bridge. These fortifications, designated the Clarence Lines, were dominated by the central gun tower, which became known as Fort Clarence.

It soon became obvious that the extent of the proposed new fortifications would demand a much larger garrison of troops to man them and plans were made to construct new barracks to relieve the pressure on the existing troop accommodation at Chatham. In 1804 construction of a new artillery and engineers' barracks at Brompton was commissioned and around the same time another new barracks was built on the Lower Lines at Gillingham. The latter site was constructed as an integral part of the fortifications with bombproof, casemated accommodation, which could also serve as gunrooms. These barracks became known as St Mary's Casemated Barracks and could accommodate up to 2,000 men.

The new barracks at Brompton were designed by James Wyatt and, in contrast to the functional appearance of St Mary's Barracks, they were once described as 'one of the largest and most impressive examples of military architecture in the country, having a compositional system ... of Palladian monumentality'. The North, South and West Blocks were built between 1804 and 1806 and originally housed 1,300 troops in dormitories with stables and gun carriage sheds nearby. Wyatt arranged the three blocks to frame a huge quadrangle, which provided a splendid backdrop for military parades. In 1812, the barracks became the home of the Royal Engineers when the School of Military Engineering was established there.

The era of the Napoleonic Wars was also an important period for renewal and improvement for the dockyard. By the 1770s many of the buildings had fallen into disrepair and in 1786 work commenced on replacing some of the most neglected buildings. The main focus of the work was at the southern end of the yard, which was almost completely rebuilt with a new fitted rigging house and storehouses along Anchor Wharf and a new double rope house. Other significant buildings that were completed in this period included the timber seasoning sheds, admirals' offices, the dockyard chapel and a steam-powered sawmill.

With the defeat of Napoleon at the Battle of Waterloo in 1815, the long-running series of wars with France came to an end and the Congress of Vienna, which had already been in session for almost a year, settled many of Europe's outstanding territorial disputes. For the first time in almost twenty-five years it seemed that Britain could now look forward to a long period of peace.

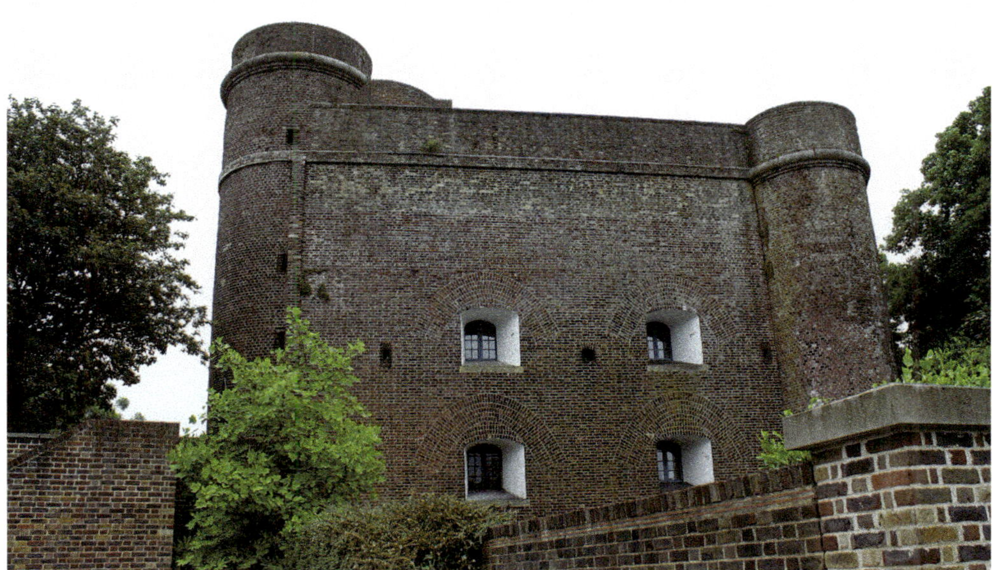

Above: The Gun Tower at Fort Clarence.

Right:
A contemporary print of Brompton Barracks as built in 1806.

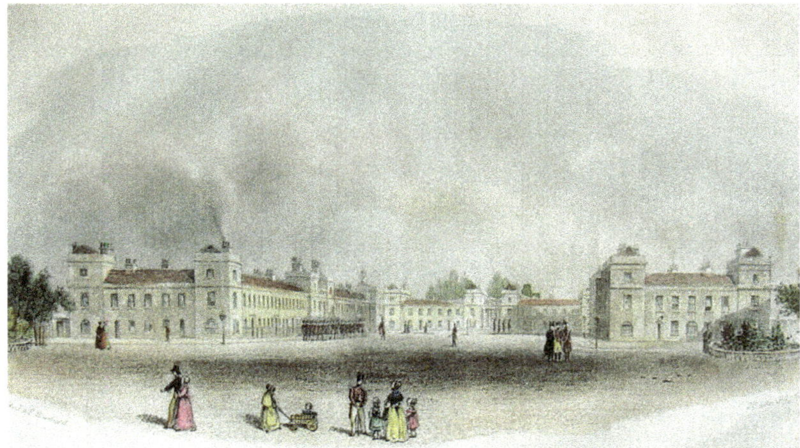

4. The Victorian Era

The years following Napoleon's defeat in 1815 were a period of decline for the British Army. With no major European campaigns to be fought, the numbers of servicemen rapidly decreased. However, with an empire to be garrisoned and occasional skirmishes with foreign tribesmen to be fought, a regular flow of new recruits would still be required.

Chatham was still an important base for the army and in 1820 its various barracks accommodated five regiments of infantry together with various detachments of artillery and engineers. By 1830 it had also become a major recruiting and training depot for regiments based overseas including those of the East India Company's army. The training was tough and what little spare time the recruits had was generally spent drinking to excess and enjoying the temptations of the neighbourhood brothels. The tensions that these excesses created with the local population and among the troops themselves often

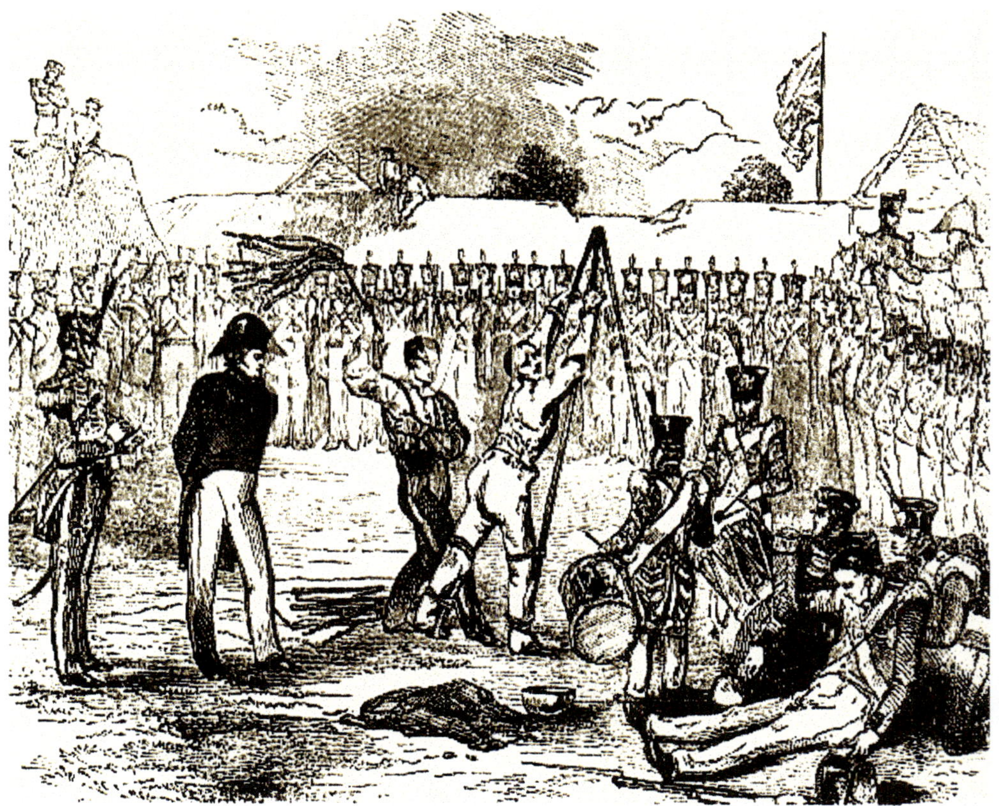

Flogging of an itinerant soldier on the Spur Battery, *c.* 1840.

resulted in vicious brawling in the streets. The army's response to such breakdowns in discipline was usually very harsh. Following a court martial an offender could look forward to punishment by flogging, which would be carried out in front his regiment. These punishments were generally carried out on the Spur Battery of Fort Amherst, with the prisoner stripped to the waist and strapped to a sturdy tripod and the flogging administered by drummers using 'cat o' nine tails'.

By the 1840s, with the increasing number of new recruits, barrack overcrowding at Chatham was becoming a serious problem contributing to major cholera outbreak in 1849. By now Chatham Military District could boast four hospitals – the Melville Naval Hospital, Fort Pitt Military Hospital, the Ordnance Hospital and Brompton Barracks Hospital – as well as an asylum that had been established at Fort Clarence. The provision of such generous medical services no doubt helped to restrict the number of deaths from the cholera epidemic to just seven servicemen.

The Chatham Lines provided ideal training grounds for the new recruits. The infantry regiments combined with engineers and artillery units to practise siege operations against the fortifications. The first major siege exercise took place in 1833 with an assault against the Duke of Cumberland's Bastion spearheaded by sappers and miners from the engineering detachments. These siege exercises soon became a regular feature along various points on the Lines and provided valuable training for any future campaigns. The siege exercises of 1849 were one of the first to attract the attention of the national press. *The Illustrated London News* of 28 July that year carried an account and drawings of the operations.

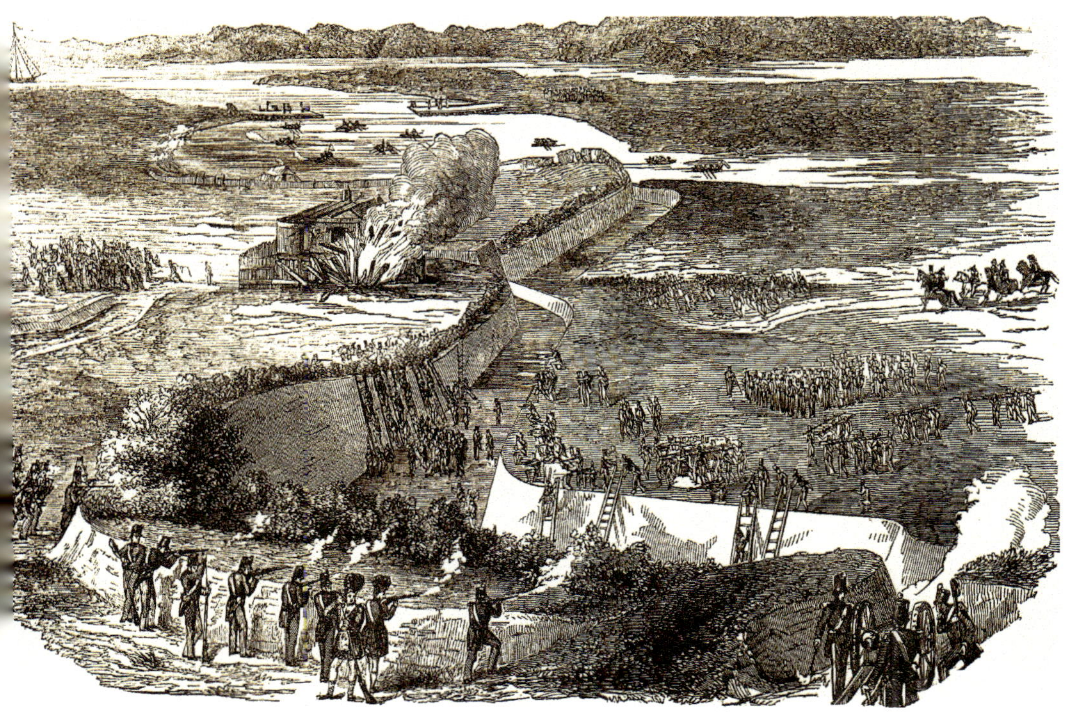

Illustrated London News article on the siege operations on the Chatham Lines in 1849.

The siege exercises were soon to prove their worth during the Crimean War, which broke out in 1853. For once Britain and France were acting together as allies in aiding the Turkish Ottoman Empire in their war with the Russian Empire. Russia had gained significant victories against the Turks in the early stages of the war and so fearing a complete Ottoman collapse, Anglo-French forces landed on the Crimean Peninsula to lay siege to the Russian Black Sea port and fortress of Sebastopol. Conditions for the troops fighting in the campaign were horrendous, even more so for the sick and wounded. Sanitation was poor, disease was rife and the medical facilities very basic. Those of the sick and wounded that managed to survive the appalling battlefield conditions were evacuated back to England where many of them were sent to convalesce at Fort Pitt Military Hospital, Chatham. Queen Victoria and Prince Albert visited the hospital in 1855 to comfort the convalescing servicemen. Their visit was documented by one of the senior doctors, William Dartnell, who had shown the royal couple around the hospital. They seemed to have left with a very good impression, as Dartnell wrote:

> *On leaving the hospital, Prince Albert said 'May I ask Mr. Dartnell if the Hospital is always as clean and nice as it is today?'*
> *I replied 'That he would find it in the same state every day of the year'*
> *'Then it is very nice indeed, nothing could be cleaner or more comfortable'*
> *… the Queen expressing gratification that no special preparations had been made for her*
> *I said that, 'I thought I should be consulting your Majesty's wishes best if I permitted you to see the Establishment in its real and every-day garb'*
> *'And you were quite right' she replied.*

Despite this royal seal of approval, just a few years later another important visit resulted in a very different conclusion. The British public had been shocked by reports of the terrible conditions faced by soldiers described by the first war correspondent of *The Times*, William Russell, and as a result in 1857 a royal commission was set up to inquire on the sanitary conditions of the army. In 1858 the commissioners visited Fort Pitt Hospital. Their report stated:

> There are no water-closets attached to this Hospital. There are very offensive privies situated on the basement, and only to be reached by passing from the sick wards into the open air, descending a flight of steps, and traversing a cold, dark, underground gallery. The privies are not drained; they are mere cesspools, the solid contents of which are removed when the vaults are full, which is the case usually once a year. The operation of cleansing usually lasts a week, and the effluvia affects the entire atmosphere of the place. The ashpit is situated in the vicinity of the privies, and close to the casemates.
>
> The whole arrangements are as bad as is possible to conceive.
>
> It is not our intention to recommend any improvements in this Hospital. It is perhaps one of the very worst places for the reception of sick in existence, and we would recommend its immediate evacuation. In fact, so bad is it, that the place should only be used for healthy men, under pressure of siege; but at no other time.

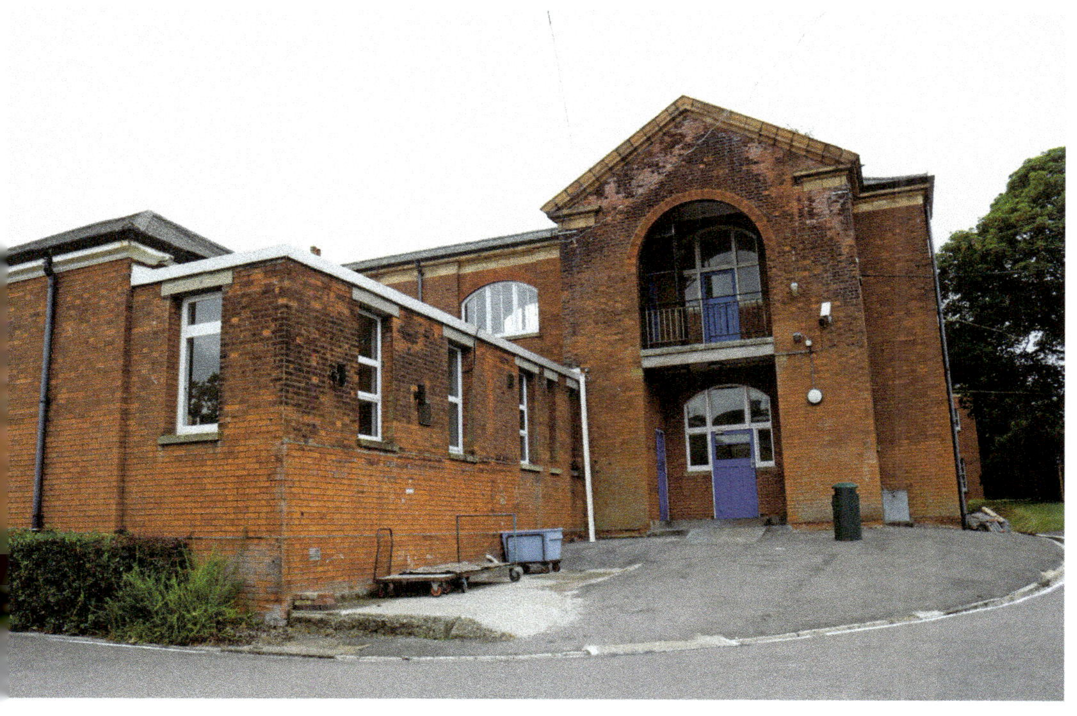

General Ward Block at Fort Pitt Military Hospital, built 1832.

However, by 1860 conditions at the hospital had improved enough for Florence Nightingale to choose it as a temporary site for the first Army Medical School. The school opened on the 2 October 1860 with the opening address being given by the Deputy Inspector-General and first Professor of Surgery, Thomas Longmore. The school moved to a new purpose-built site at the Royal Victoria Hospital, Netley, in 1863, with Fort Pitt continuing to operate as a military hospital for another sixty years.

As well as the bad medical conditions, the Crimean War had found other aspects of Britain's war-making machine seriously wanting. The Board of Ordnance, which had been responsible for the supply of munitions and equipment to both the army and the navy, were heavily criticised for their poor performance during the war and especially for their lack of preparedness to cope with the conditions of the Russian winter of 1854, which resulted in a complete breakdown of transport and hospital arrangements over the period. As a consequence of these failings, the board was disbanded and its myriad responsibilities split between the War Department and the Admiralty, with the board's site at Chatham Gun Wharf being handed to the War Department. In the 1860s the northern part of the Gun Wharf site from the defensive Barrier Ditch to the boundary with the Royal Dockyard was transferred to the Admiralty while the remainder was retained by the War Department. The Navy Gun Wharf, with its Grand Storehouse, stored cannon and munitions for use on HM ships while the Army Gun Wharf (also known as the New Gun Wharf) continued in use as an arsenal and storehouse for the forts.

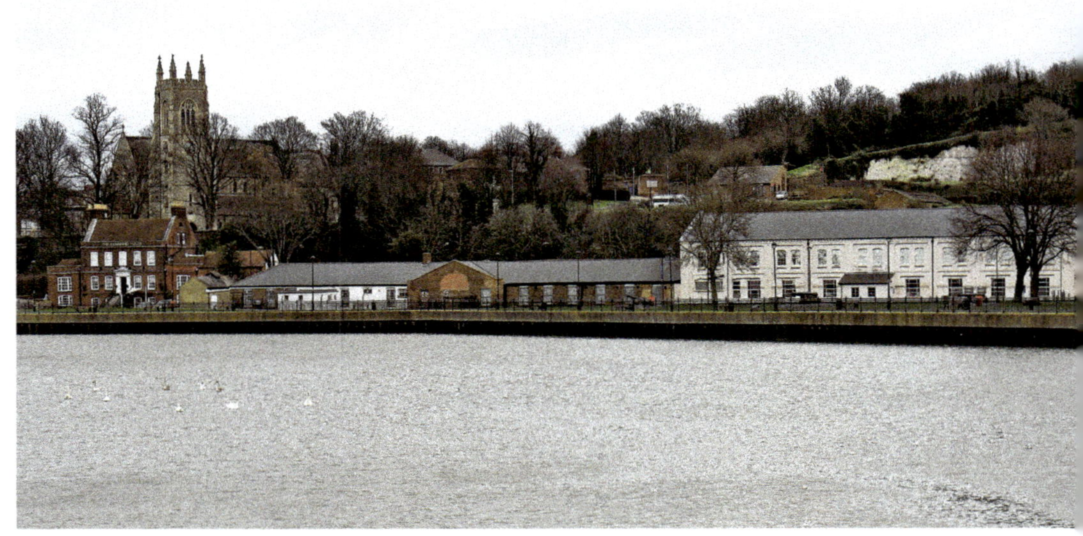

The Gun Wharf site in 2014.

The War Department also took over the ordnance depot at Upnor and with it the supply of munitions to the Royal Navy's warships based at Chatham as well as the needs of the army manning its outlying fortifications. They soon deemed Upnor's facilities inadequate to cope with these demands and in 1871 a committee was formed by order of the Inspector General of Fortifications to report on a site for a proposed new magazine for the Medway District. The decision was taken to build a new storage compound to hold 40,000 barrels of gunpowder further inland on the Hoo Peninsula at nearby Chattenden. The compound would consist of five magazines holding 8,000 barrels each. The magazines were completed in June 1875 by convict labour and were set into a traversed hillside, which caused slippages during construction.

The magazines were connected to the Chattenden Barracks, which had been completed in 1872 to provide accommodation for eight officers and 120 soldiers to guard the compound, by a railway that ran south to Upnor. This railway was originally built as a standard-gauge line to transport building materials for the construction of the new magazines and barracks from the wharf at Upnor. By the 1880s the standard-gauge line was abandoned, and the tracks lifted to be replaced with a 2-foot 6-inch narrow-gauge line to transport munitions. This line became known as the Chattenden & Upnor Railway. A tramway was also constructed, which ran eastwards to Hoo Creek.

By the mid-nineteenth century new technologies such as iron and steam had been introduced into shipbuilding at the dockyard. New slips, docks, workshops and smitheries had been built to handle these new processes but with the ever-increasing size of the Royal Navy and its warships, the demands on the dockyard were rapidly outgrowing its facilities.

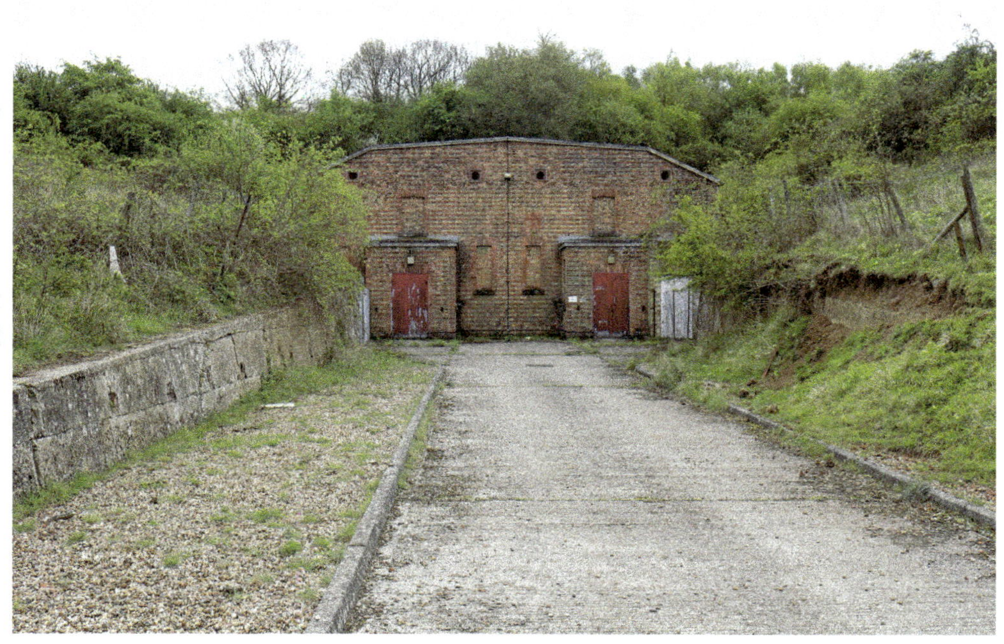

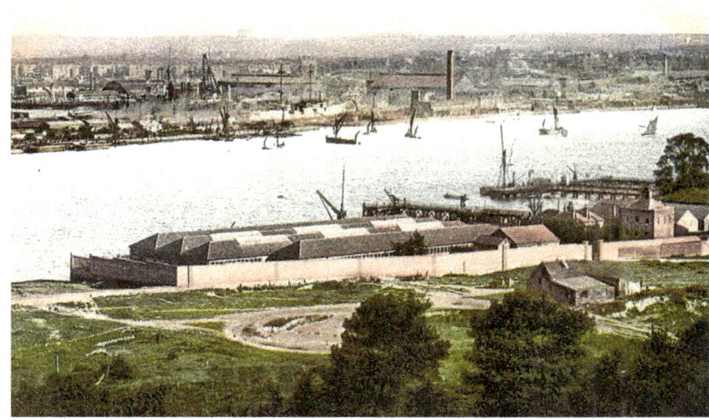

Above: One of the Chattenden magazines.

Right: Upnor Ordnance Depot looking across to the dockyard, *c.* 1880.

In the early 1860s work commenced on a massive expansion and modernisation of the yard, which would add 380 acres to its existing 97 acres. Most of the new work was concentrated on St Mary's Island to the north of the yard. The marshland there was drained ready for the construction of three huge new basins. Eventually five new docks and a new building slip were incorporated into the expansion together with numerous new workshops, pumping stations, storehouses and a railway system. Most of the labour force for the construction of the dockyard extension was drawn from the convict population. Convicts had been housed on insanitary old naval hulks moored on the Medway and used for construction jobs in the

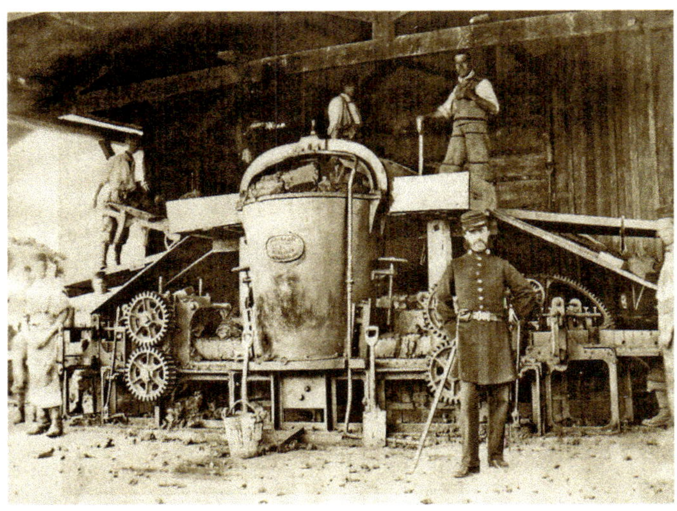

Convicts manning a brick-making machine on the dockyard extension works.

dockyard for many years, but in 1850 a new purpose-built prison had opened on St Mary's Island to house up to 1,000 convicts in conditions far superior than those they had endured on the hulks. However, despite the improved conditions, in 1861 a mutiny broke out in the prison that had to be put down with the help of 400 Chatham-based Royal Marines.

Despite their brief alliance during the Crimean War, Britain's relationship with France continued to be strained. Under Napoleon III France had sought to reassert its influence in Europe and overseas, doubling the size of the French Empire in Africa, Asia and the Pacific and threatening Britain's interests in those regions. Worries again surfaced in Britain about a possible French invasion. The 1850s had seen some improvements in the outlying defences of Chatham including the construction of a Martello-like gun tower in the mouth of the Medway between Grain and Sheerness. However, the development by the French of steam-powered warships with rifled guns, giving them much greater range, caused the greatest concern to the British.

A royal commission was set up in 1860 to review national defence and its recommendations included construction of a new 'outer-ring' of forts to defend Chatham Dockyard. Five new forts were built to the south of Chatham and named Forts Borstal, Bridgewoods, Horsted, Luton and Darland. As an experimental project the Royal Engineers also constructed new-style fortifications to the south of the Medway near the village of Twydall to protect the right flank of the new outer ring of forts. Named Woodland Redoubt and Grange Redoubt, they were designed from experience gained of Turkish fortifications during the Crimean War. Another two new forts were to be constructed on islands in the Medway, which became known as Fort Hoo and Fort Darnet. Further afield on the Hoo Peninsula new forts and gun batteries were built at Allhallows (Slough Fort) and Grain (Grain Fort and Grain Battery) to defend against landings from the Thames Estuary.

Due to a lack of money construction of the new forts didn't commence until the 1870s and by the 1880s further new developments in the range and power of artillery were already making them obsolete. It was not until 1900, forty years since it was first proposed, that the Chatham Outer-Ring Fortress was eventually completed, by which time it was no longer fit for the purpose it was originally designed for.

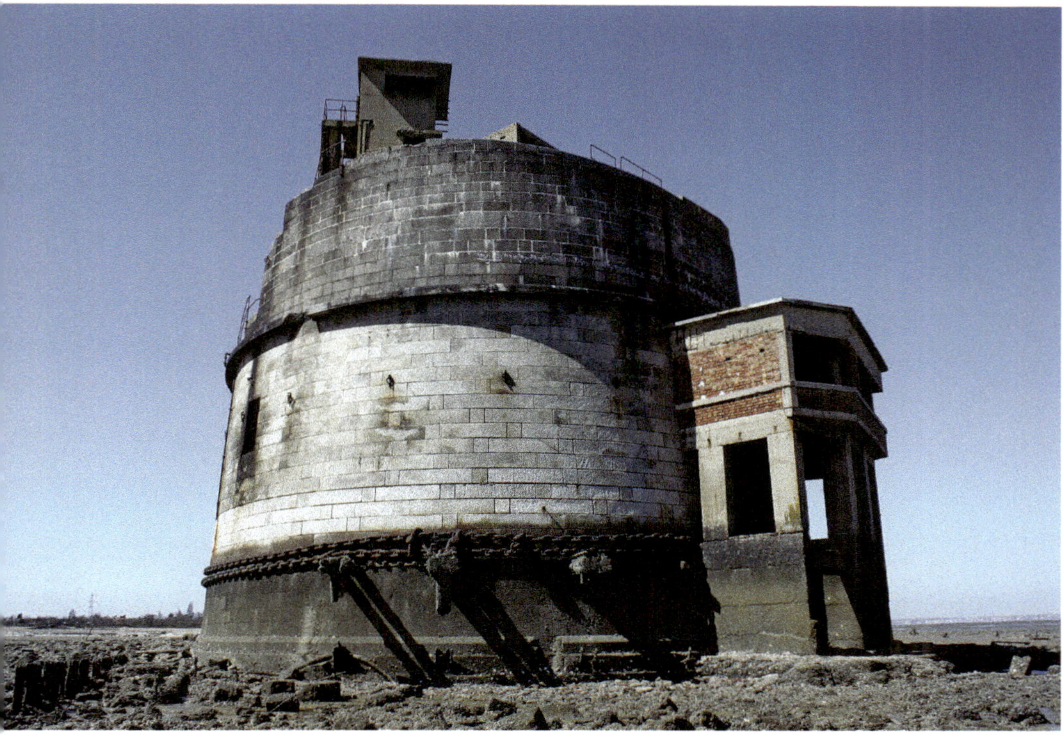

Grain Tower Battery defended the entrance to the River Medway.

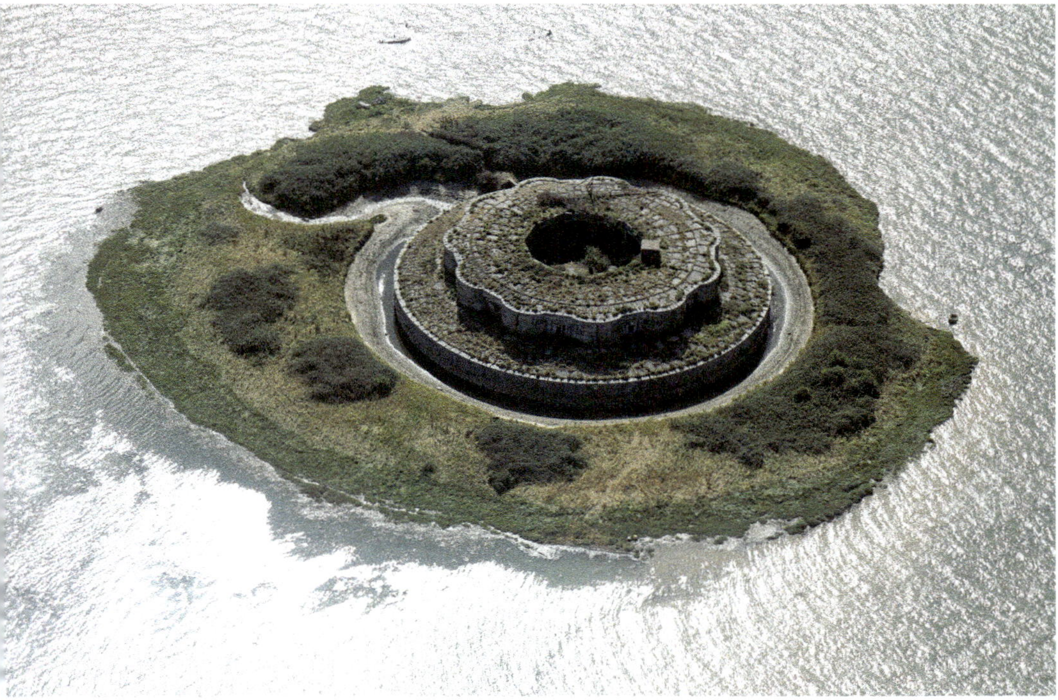

Fort Darnet.

5. World Wars

The early years of the twentieth century saw Chatham renewed as a powerful naval and military base. The vast extension to the dockyard was completed in 1903 with the opening of No. 9 Dock. At 650 feet in length, it was at that time the longest dock in the world and capable of handling the navy's largest warships.

That same year the new Royal Naval Barracks, HMS *Pembroke*, opened on the site of the demolished convict prison, replacing the old hulks moored in No. 2 Basin which, until then, had served as accommodation ships for the seamen based at Chatham. The barracks provided accommodation for 4,700 officers and men, a figure that could be more than doubled during wartime. As well as the accommodation blocks and messes, the barracks included a Drill Shed, Gunnery School, and indoor swimming baths. In 1906, the building of a new barrack church was completed and dedicated to St George. Another later addition was the Gymnasium, which was completed in 1908 and provided a purpose-built indoor facility with the latest gym equipment to keep the servicemen at peak fitness all-year round.

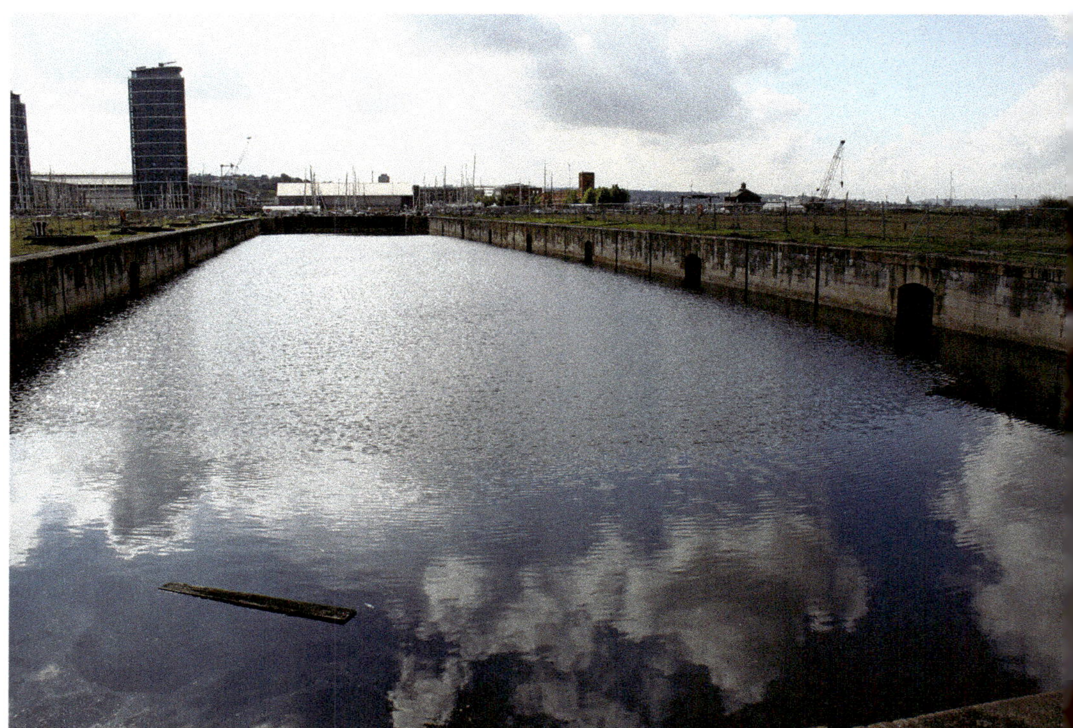

No. 9 Dock, Chatham Dockyard, completed in 1903.

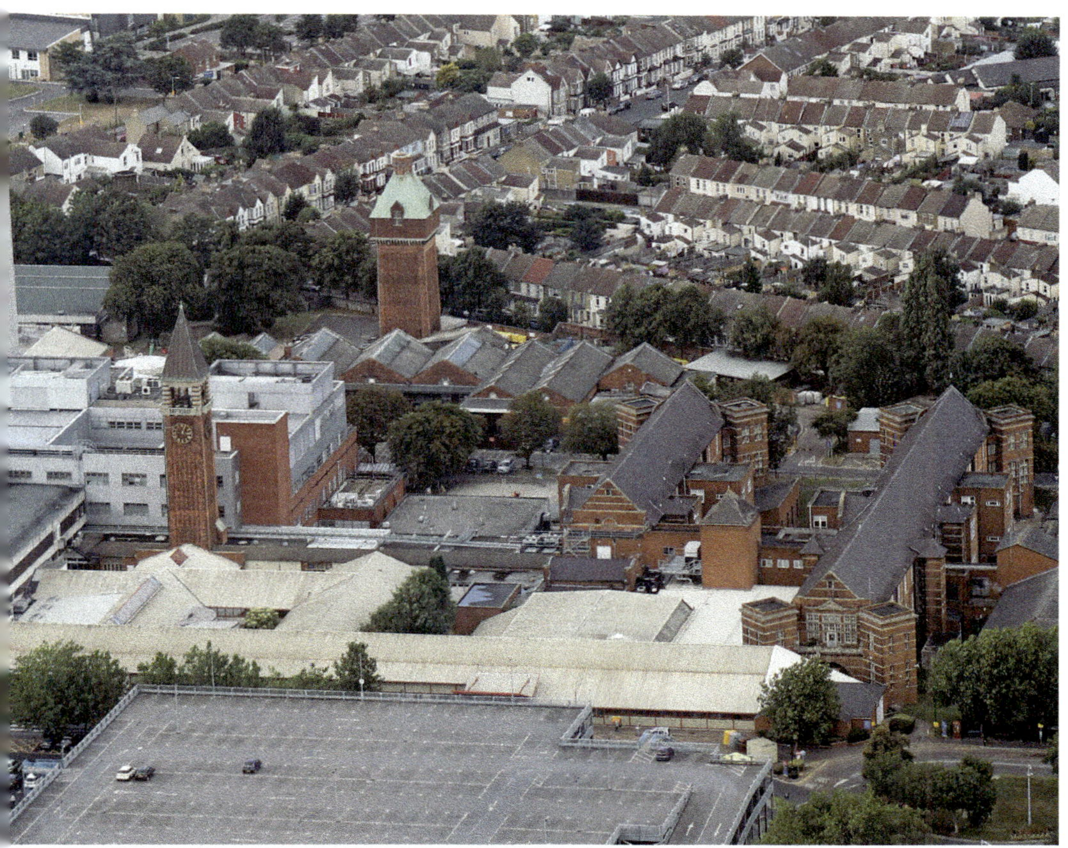

Aerial photo of the former Chatham Royal Navy Hospital, now Medway Maritime Hospital.

To serve the new barracks a naval hospital was built on the Great Lines at Gillingham. It was opened by Edward VII in 1905 and was designated as Royal Naval Hospital Chatham. The king carried out the opening ceremony using a gold key presented to him in a silver casket. He then toured the hospital's wards, operating theatres and kitchens.

In 1891, the Admiralty took over the responsibility for supplying armaments to the fleet from the War Office. However, the army retained the magazines at Chattenden, together with the railway line, for their own use, thus the navy found itself short of accommodation for its own armaments. Following the submission of several reports, in 1898 the decision was taken to purchase 500 acres of land at Lodge Hill, adjacent to the Chattenden compound, from the War Office for £16,000. Initial plans were drawn up to build two cordite magazines, each of 40,000 cubic feet, three explosive stores of 40,000 cubic feet, one dry cotton store, and two examining rooms and one deposit magazine. By 1904 five cordite magazines had been completed, as had the guncotton store, the deposit magazine for explosives received from ships, and three explosive stores. In 1903, the Admiralty took over the older Chattenden Magazine Enclosure and in 1906 they also took over control of the Chattenden & Upnor Railway from the army.

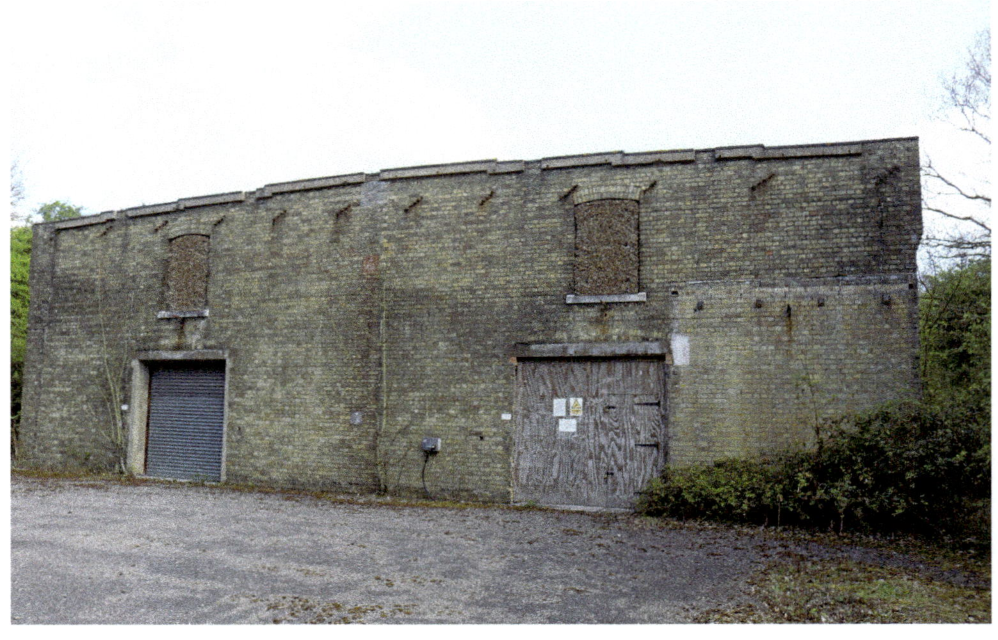

Cordite Store at Lodge Hill.

In 1911, the Royal Navy's magazines at Chattenden and Lodge Hill came to the attention of the then Home Secretary, Winston Churchill. In early April that year a rebellion broke out in Morocco against its Sultan. The French government, under whose 'sphere of influence' the North African kingdom came, prepared to send troops to put down the rebellion and protect European lives. They despatched a column of troops to Fez in late April despite pleas from the British government to show restraint. Meanwhile the German government ordered their gunboat the *Panther* to the Moroccan port of Agadir and she docked there on 1 July, raising tensions with the French. The British were also concerned that the Germans intended to take advantage of the crisis to create a naval base on Morocco's Atlantic coast and so, albeit grudgingly, pledged their support to France. Meanwhile Churchill, who as Home Secretary was in charge of the Metropolitan Police who in turn were responsible for guarding the Royal Navy's stores of cordite at Lodge Hill and Chattenden, was dining with the Metropolitan Police Commissioner. Inquiring of him the preparedness of the police guards in the event of a surprise German raid on the magazines, he was shocked to be told they were not issued with firearms. Both the First Lord of the Admiralty and the First Sea Lord were away and out of contact, so Churchill made an urgent call to the local naval Commander-in-Chief to request armed Royal Marine guards for the magazines. This request was refused, so he then contacted the Minister of War, who immediately agreed the despatch of two companies of infantry to the magazines. At the same time Churchill authorized the issuing of firearms to the magazines' Metropolitan Police guards. Churchill's worst fears were never realised and the crisis abated with the signing of the Treaty of Fez in November 1911, by which time Churchill himself had become First Lord of the Admiralty.

Imperial Germany had now replaced France as the greatest threat to Britain. The Kaiser was intent on building a fleet capable of challenging the Royal Navy and the two countries engaged in a 'naval race' to build the greatest number of the fast, heavily armed and armoured *Dreadnought* type of battleship. Britain had launched the first of these revolutionary new ships in 1906 and by 1914 the Royal Navy had twenty-two afloat against Germany's fifteen. However, none of this new class of battleships had been built at Chatham. With a minimum displacement of 18,000 tons they were far too large for Chatham's building facilities. The dockyard had built its last battleship, HMS *Africa*, in 1905 and was now specialising in the building of submarines and destroyers.

When the First World War broke out in August 1914 the Chatham Division of the Royal Navy consisted of 205 ships of various types and the Medway anchorage was full of vessels on standby ready to be called into action. Many of them had been at anchor there for years on reserve including the five old *Cressy*-class cruisers of the 7th Squadron. The day war was declared the 7th Cruiser Squadron left Chatham and headed for the North Sea. On the morning of 22 September three of the ships, *Aboukir*, *Cressy* and *Hogue*, were sunk by a single German submarine and 1,500 of their crew perished. It was Chatham's first major tragedy of the war. This was soon followed by another when on 26 November the battleship *Bulwark* blew up while moored in the Medway off Sheerness with a number of Chatham-based ratings on board. The cause of the explosion was accidental, aided by a design fault common in that class of battleship.

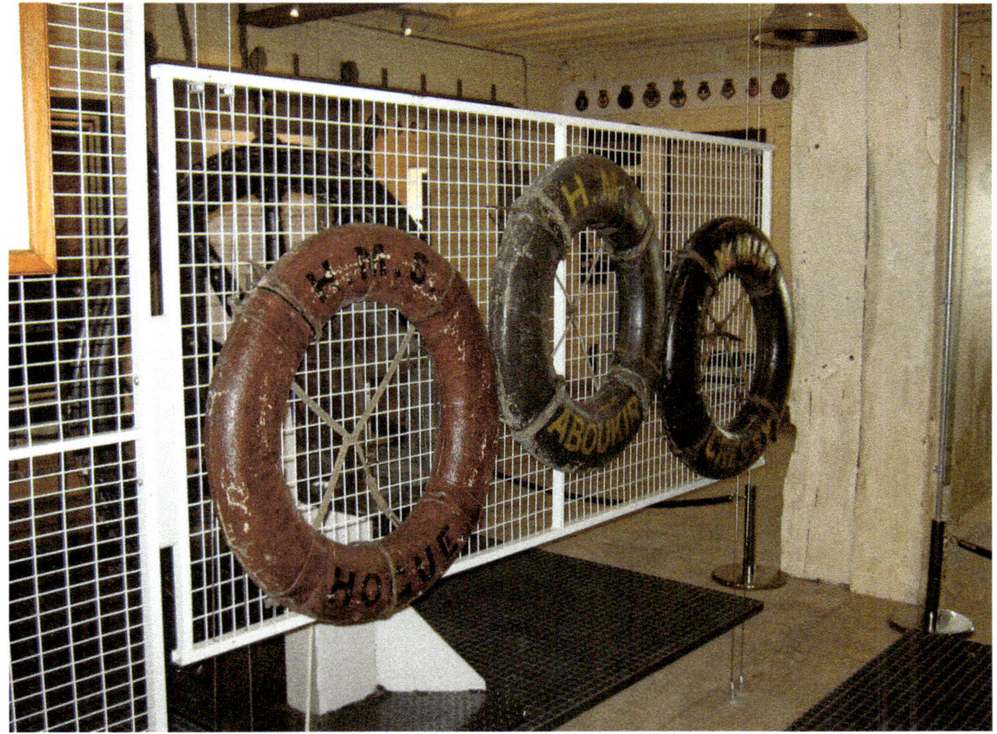

Lifebelts from *Aboukir*, *Cressy* and *Hogue* on display at Chatham Dockyard Museum.

As well as at sea threats also came from the air. With their advance into France and Belgium, the Germans now had aircraft and airships within bombing range of Chatham. The ordnance depots at Lodge Hill and Chattenden were at high risk of attack. One of the world's first anti-aircraft batteries was built on the high ground at Lodge Hill and another on Beacon Hill to provide the depots with defence against aerial bombing. On the night of 3 September 1917, four German Gotha bombers struck at the Medway Towns. One bomb fell on the Drill Shed at Royal Naval Barracks, which was at the time being used as overflow accommodation for seamen from the sunken battleship HMS *Vanguard*, who were awaiting reassignment to other ships. Over 900 men were sleeping when the 1,000 lb bomb fell through the glass roof of the Drill Shed before exploding on the concrete floor below. The final death toll was 126 with many more seriously injured.

Soon after the outbreak of the war, Minister of War Lord Kitchener appealed for volunteers to boost the strength of Britain's relatively small professional army. Millions rallied to his call and collectively became known as 'Kitchener's New Army'. It became a matter of urgency to get these new recruits trained ready to join the front line in France.

In August 1914 a new infantry training unit known as No. 1 Training Depot Battalion was formed and based on the Great Lines at Chatham. The battalion consisted of 6,000 men, 2,000 of whom were housed in the existing Chatham Barracks with the rest accommodated in a temporary camp of tents and huts set up on the Lines. In just over a year, the training depot had supplied some 29,000 NCOs and men for reinforcements to the British Expeditionary Force in France.

As can be imagined, during the war Fort Pitt Military Hospital was a very busy establishment treating hundreds of wounded British, Allied and German servicemen. Many of those that the hospital could not save were buried in the nearby Fort Pitt Military Cemetery.

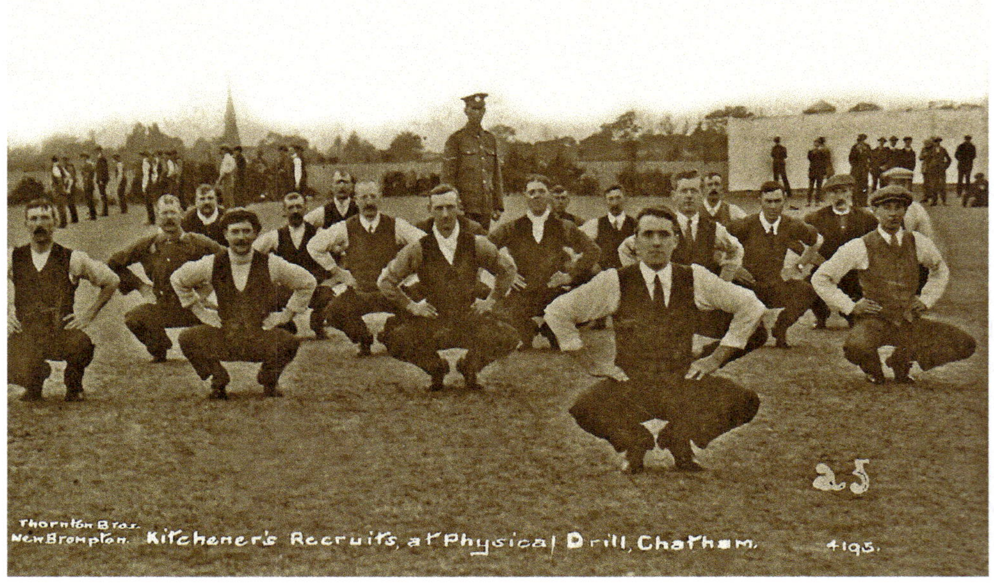

Recruits of Kitchener's 'New Army' training on the Great Lines.

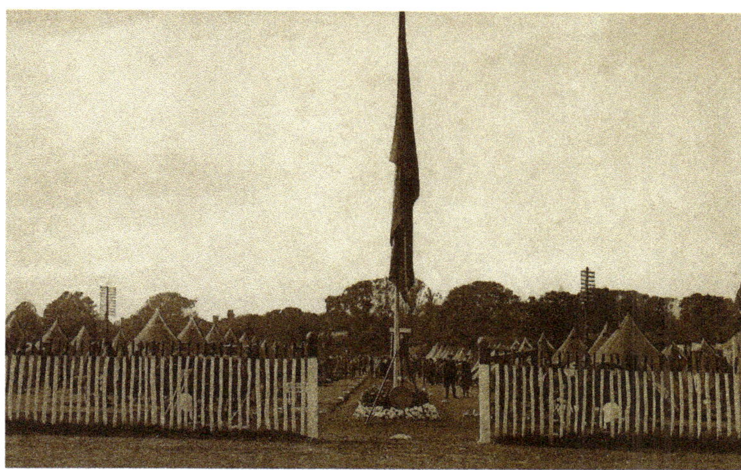

No. 1 Training Depot Camp on the Great Lines in 1915.

The end of the First World War saw a rapid decline of its military and naval establishment. Chatham Dockyard, which by 1918 was employing over 11,000 people, was particularly badly affected with the cancellation of orders for the building of many ships and submarines no longer required leading to the laying-off of thousands of workers.

Chatham's army garrison was also greatly rundown as thousands of conscripts were demobbed, local forts and defences were abandoned, and barracks emptied. However, there was some new investment at the Chatham Infantry Barracks where many of the original eighteenth-century buildings were demolished to be replaced with modern barrack accommodation. The barracks were taken over by the Royal Engineers and renamed as Kitchener Barracks in honour of the late Minister of War and former student at the Chatham School of Military Engineering Field Marshall Lord Kitchener, who had drowned at sea in the First World War.

Fort Pitt Military Hospital was closed in 1919 and in the 1930s work began on the demolition of much of the original fort to make way for the construction of a new Girls' Grammar School.

By the mid-1930s Germany, under Adolf Hitler, was a resurgent military power determined to restore the lands lost in the wake of its defeat in the First World War. After a period of many years starving its armed forces of funds, Britain began rearming. The principle benefactor of new investment was the RAF, which embarked on a major programme of expansion of its squadrons and airfields to counter the threat from the German Air Force. The threat from the air also resulted in a number of major new underground works in the Chatham District including the construction of deep-level air-raid shelters at the various barrack sites and a new underground HQ for the Royal Navy's Nore Command.

The 1930s also saw a small revival of the dockyard's shipbuilding activities. In 1935, the cruiser HMS *Arethusa* was launched from No. 8 Slip and her place was taken a year later when work commenced on constructing her sister ship *Euryalus*. As well as the cruisers, increased orders were being placed for the construction of new submarines. When completed, all these new vessels would require fitting-out and ongoing maintenance, so the numbers of workers employed at the dockyard steadily increased.

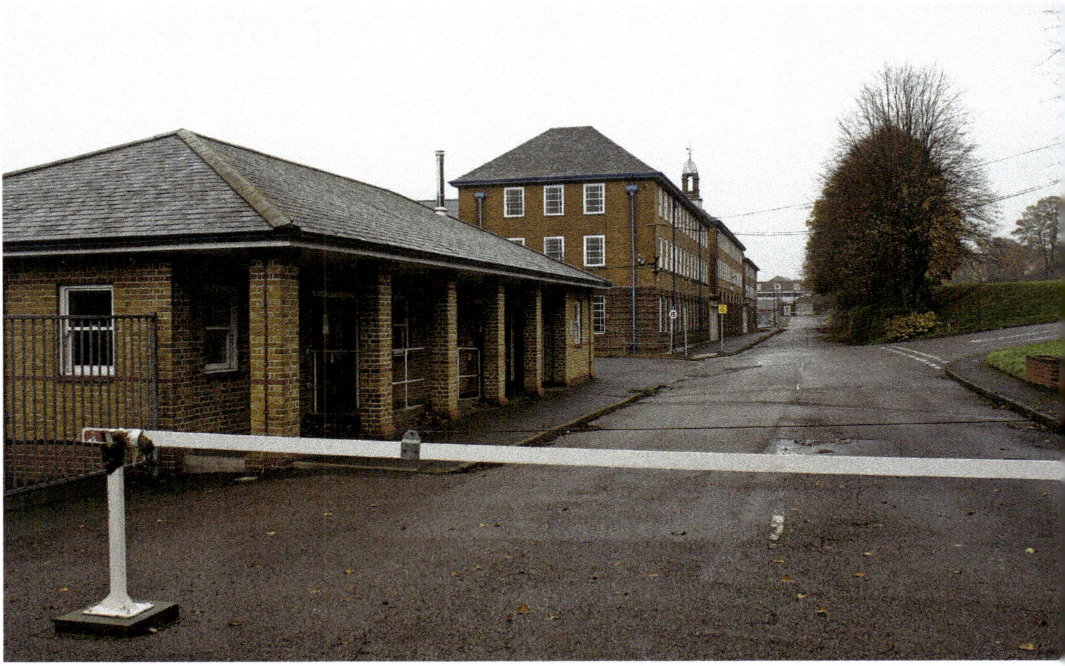

Kitchener Barracks in 2015.

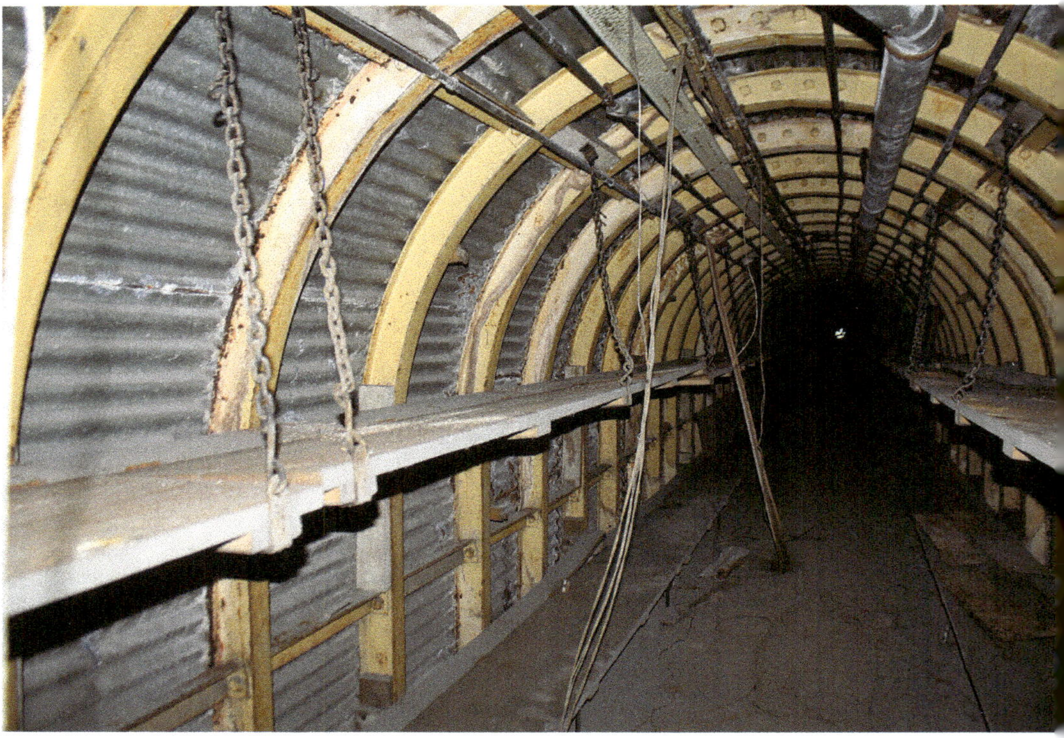

The Royal Marines Barracks Deep Shelter.

When war eventually broke out again in 1939, Chatham had to cope with a mass influx of extra servicemen in the form of those being called up from reserve as well as thousands of newly conscripted recruits. The existing barrack accommodation was soon stretched to its limits and new hutted camps began to appear to cope with the overflows.

Many of the old Napoleonic and Victorian era forts were adapted for new roles. Fort Luton became the Gun Operations Room for the 27th Anti-Aircraft Brigade covering the Thames and Medway District; the gun emplacements at Fort Borstal were converted to house the 4.5-inch guns of the 166 City of Rochester Heavy Anti-Aircraft Battery; Fort Horsted also mounted anti-aircraft guns; Fort Bridgewoods became a secret out-station of Bletchley Park, intercepting coded German wireless transmissions; and the tunnels at Fort Amherst were taken over by the Civil Defence for use as their Medway headquarters.

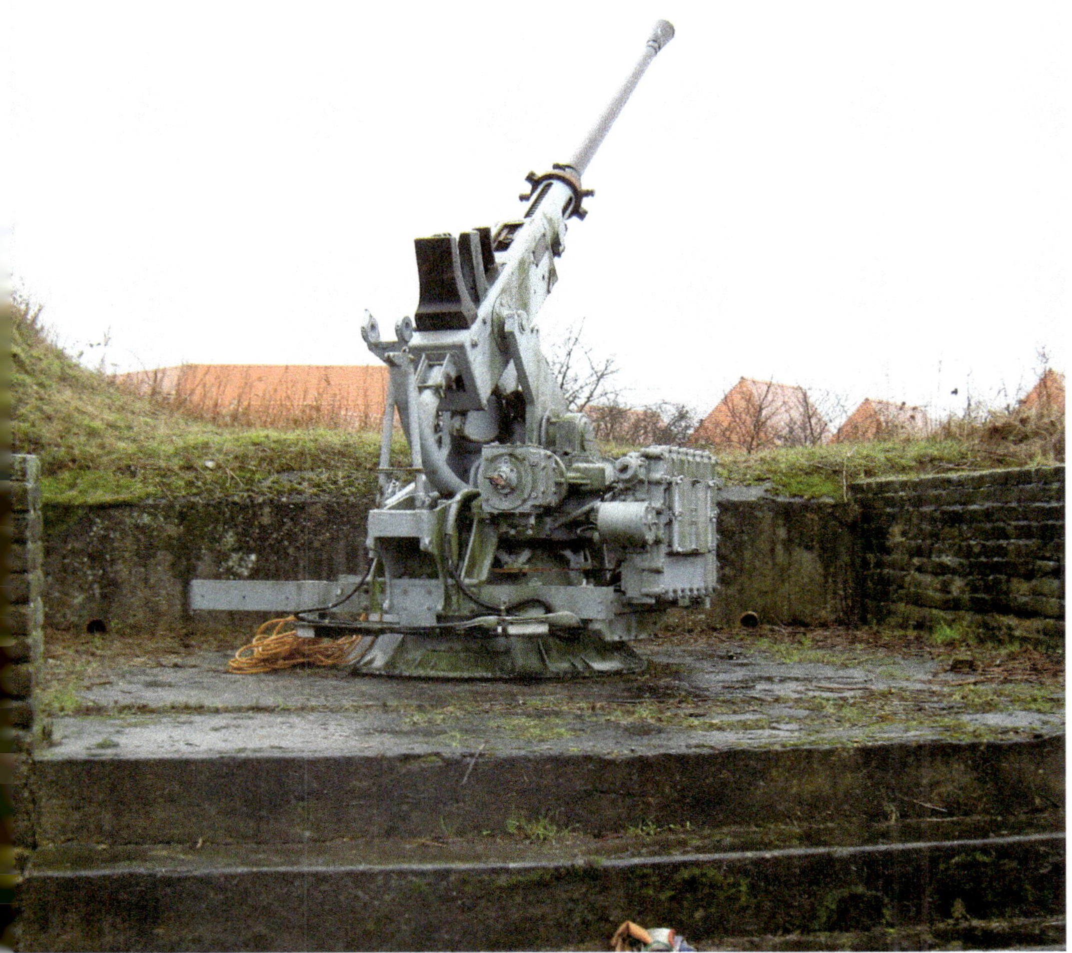

Second World War anti-aircraft gun emplacement at Fort Horsted.

The old defence works of the Chatham Lines were augmented with new gun positions, trenches, anti-tank obstacles and pillboxes and a comprehensive anti-invasion plan was drawn up for the Chatham Garrison. The Chatham and Rochester Home Guard battalions were an integral part of this plan and were tasked with manning most of the area's 600 plus roadblocks as well as anti-tank and anti-aircraft gun positions. The dockyard boasted its own Home Guard battalion, membership of which eventually became compulsory for all male dockyard workers, making it the largest single battalion in Kent.

The dockyard played a very important role throughout the war, maintaining, refitting and repairing over 1,300 vessels as well as constructing twelve submarines, four sloops and two floating docks. At the war's height the yard employed 13,000 workers, 2,000 of whom were women. Following Germany's defeat the dockyard was engaged in refitting part of the fleet destined to engage in the final throes of the war against Japan in the Pacific.

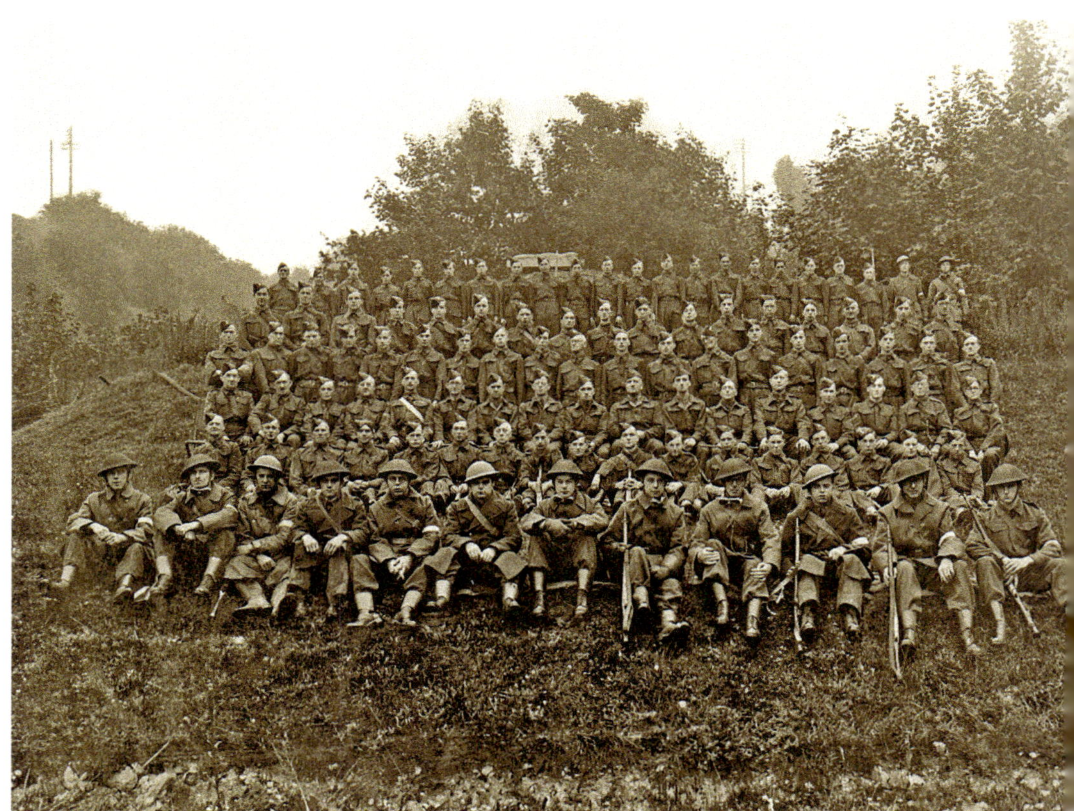

The 12th (Chatham) Battalion, Kent Home Guard.

6. A Long Sunset

Following the end of the Second World War, Britain found itself heavily in debt. The new Labour government was under great pressure to cut budgets while simultaneously honouring its manifesto commitments on setting up the National Health Service and nationalising key industries. The armed forces were an obvious target for severe spending cuts and with millions of servicemen and women being demobilised, many barracks, depots, airfields and naval bases were deemed surplus to requirements. The dockyard at Chatham soon found itself with an uncertain future and its work levels dramatically reduced. Many of those recruited to work in the yard during the hostilities were discharged including most of the 2,000 female workers. The emergency entrances to the dockyard in Dock Road, built to cope with the huge wartime workforce, were sealed up and to keep the remaining workers occupied, the yard was obligated to supplement its reduced naval work with civilian contracts.

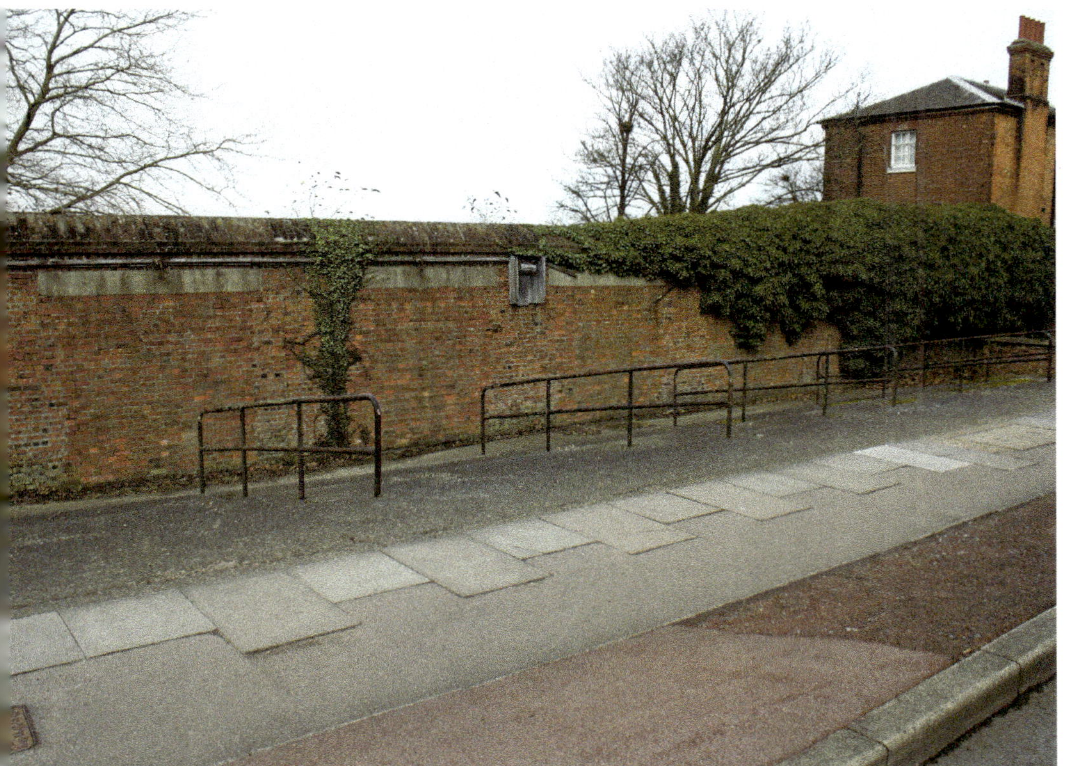

Emergency wartime dockyard entrances sealed up at the end of the war.

Among the post-war casualties effecting Chatham's military establishment were the closures of the army's Southill Barracks on the Maidstone Road and St Mary's Barracks on the Lower Lines at Gillingham; but probably the greatest blow was the announcement of the abolition of the Royal Marines Chatham Division and the closure of its barracks on Dock Road. The announcement of the closure was made to Parliament in March 1950 and in a 'Special Order of the Day' dated 23 March 1950, Lieutenant-General L. C. Hollis, Commandant General of the Royal Marines, said, 'Chatham is our oldest home. We have been there since 1708 and have recently been honoured by the granting of the Freedom of the Borough. Although some Royal Marines will remain in Chatham, we are vacating the main barracks, which have been ours since about 1780.' The barracks closed on 31 August 1950, leaving just a small rear party and Chatham Group HQ behind, but by 1 November these too were gone.

The army and Royal Navy continued to use the Gun Wharf, adjacent to the Royal Marines Barracks, after the war. The Royal Army Ordnance Corps (RAOC) Research and Development Centre moved there in 1946 and was renamed the RAOC Field Test Centre. It was also an outstation of the Chemical Inspectorate at Woolwich Arsenal. The dawn of the nuclear age saw this latter organisation incorporated into the newly founded Atomic Energy Research Establishment (AERE), which leased some buildings on the Gun Wharf where they engaged in research on beryllium metals used in nuclear bomb triggers. The Royal Navy finally vacated the Gun Wharf in 1958 and the whole site along with the Royal Marines Barracks was put up for sale. All the Royal Marine Barracks and most of the Gun Wharf was demolished in the 1960s, leaving just a few buildings from the latter as a reminder of a once bustling military and naval presence.

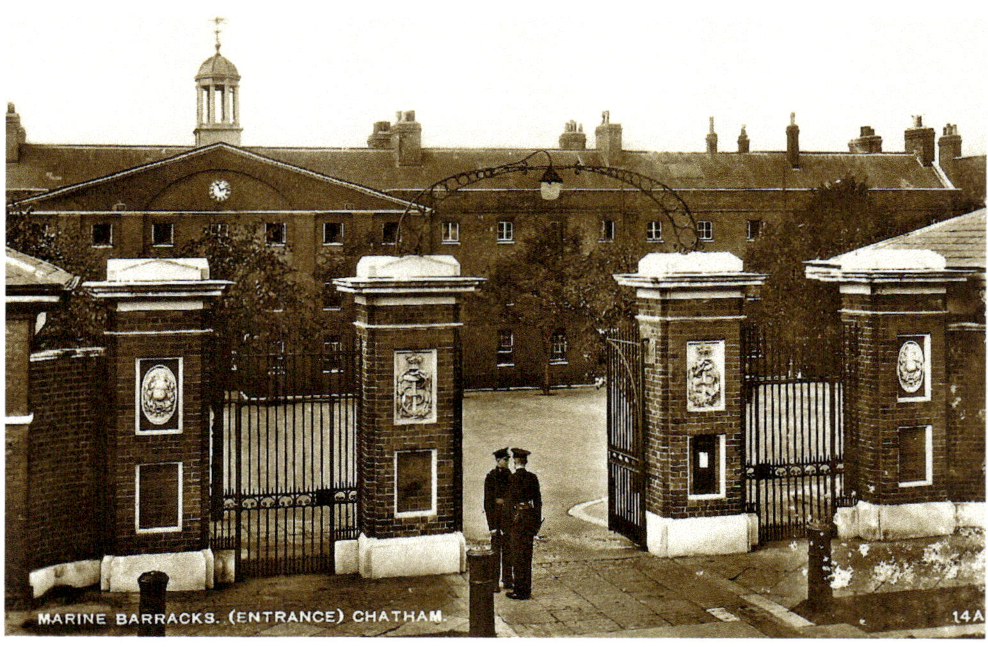

The Royal Marines Barracks *c.* 1920.

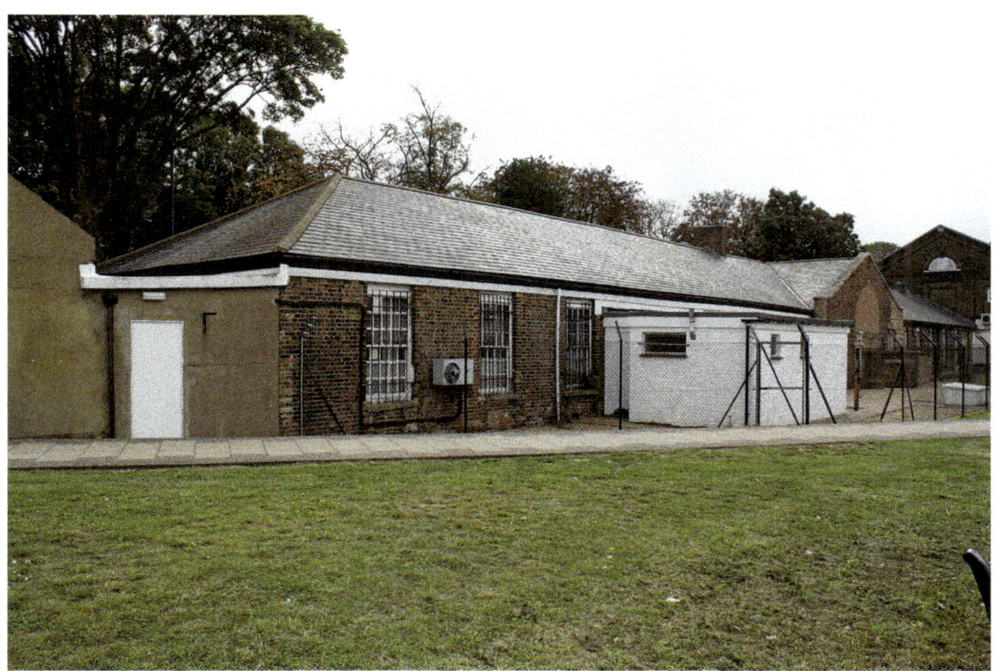

The former Armoury at the Gun Wharf in 2015.

Despite the cutbacks and the loss of India to the British Empire, the United Kingdom in the 1950s remained a great military power with global commitments. The Royal Navy was still one of the largest navies in the world and much of its submarine force was maintained and refitted at Chatham Dockyard.

On 12 January 1950, the submarine HMS *Truculent*, having completed a refit at Chatham, was returning to her base at Sheerness with eighteen dockyard workers still aboard her in addition to her normal crew when she collided with the Swedish oil tanker *Divina* in the Thames Estuary. The submarine sank rapidly to the seabed 80 feet below. Most of those on board survived the initial collision and managed to close the watertight doors to the damaged compartments. The survivors were split into two groups, which then occupied the sealed engine room and Engineers' Mess compartments. Unfortunately, although there were enough escape sets for everyone on board, they were spread throughout the boat. Those sets that were readily available were given to the weakest swimmers and the order was given to flood the compartments and open the escape hatch. All the survivors left the submarine in an orderly fashion and made it to the surface. Unfortunately, the *Divina* had not notified the Admiralty about the collision as her radio was not working, so no rescue vessels were there to meet them and most of the men were swept away by the strong currents. In the end, of the seventy-nine men on board only fifteen survivors were rescued with sixty-four perishing in the freezing waters of the estuary.

As well as boats from the submarine fleet, the dockyard played a very active role in the refitting and maintenance of surface vessels from the Royal Navy's Nore Command. These were mostly from the smaller classes of ships such as destroyers and patrol vessels,

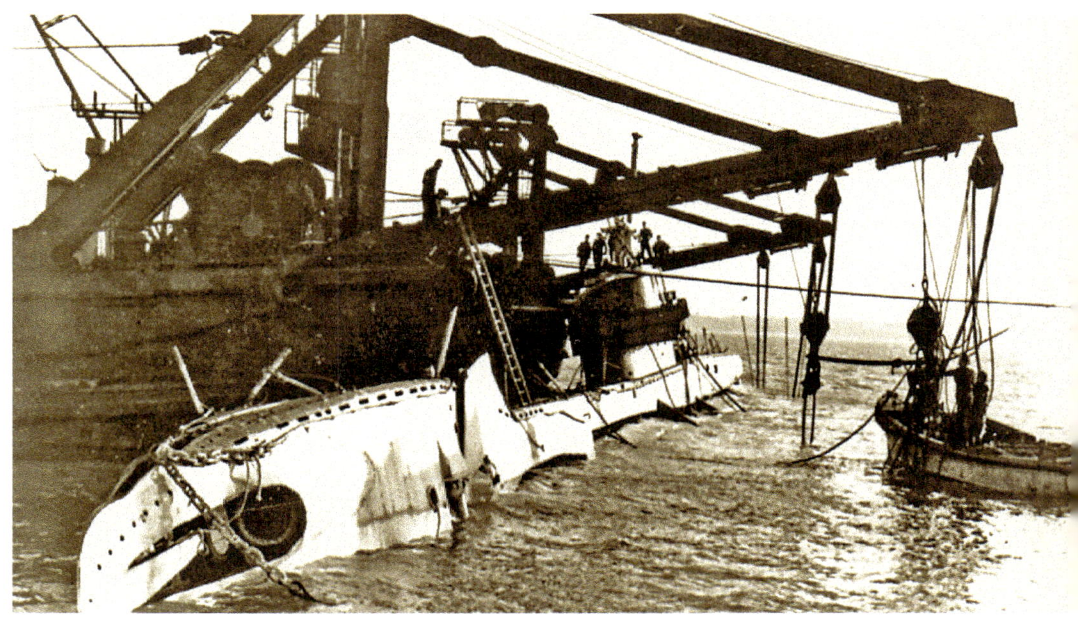

The raising of HMS *Truculent*.

but occasionally the yard was called upon to work on larger ships. One of these was the former wartime escort carrier HMS *Campania*. In 1952, she entered No. 9 Dock to be fitted out as the flagship for the first British nuclear bomb tests at Monte Bello Islands, off the coast of Western Australia. Another vessel based at Chatham at the time was the frigate HMS *Plym*, which was also to be involved with the nuclear bomb tests. It was her unfortunate task to be used as the detonation platform for the bomb. On 3 October 1952 a 25-kiloton device was detonated on the vessel, obliterating her completely.

The immediate post-war decades saw the Royal Engineers being deployed in conflicts across the globe including those in Palestine, Korea, Suez, Malaya and South Arabia. As the Cold War intensified, British military policy became increasingly focused on Germany and by the late 1960s the corps was committed to supporting the British Army of Rhine with up to seven regiments, and their supporting network of logistic support based in West Germany. Most of the sappers involved in those operations would have received their training at the School of Military Engineering at Brompton, which, in 1962, in recognition of the 150th anniversary of its foundation, was renamed the Royal School of Military Engineering (RSME). In 1961, the school took over the Royal Naval Armaments Depots at Lodge Hill and Chattenden and both areas became training sites for bridging and construction techniques as well as home to the Joint Service Bomb Disposal School.

In 1966, these sites were supplemented with the opening of the new purpose-built Lodge Hill Camp and the Bomb Disposal School renamed the Defence Explosive Ordnance Disposal School (DEODS). This training facility became invaluable when, from 1969, sectarian unrest in Northern Ireland increasingly turned into violent terrorist conflict with bomb attacks against British forces in the Province.

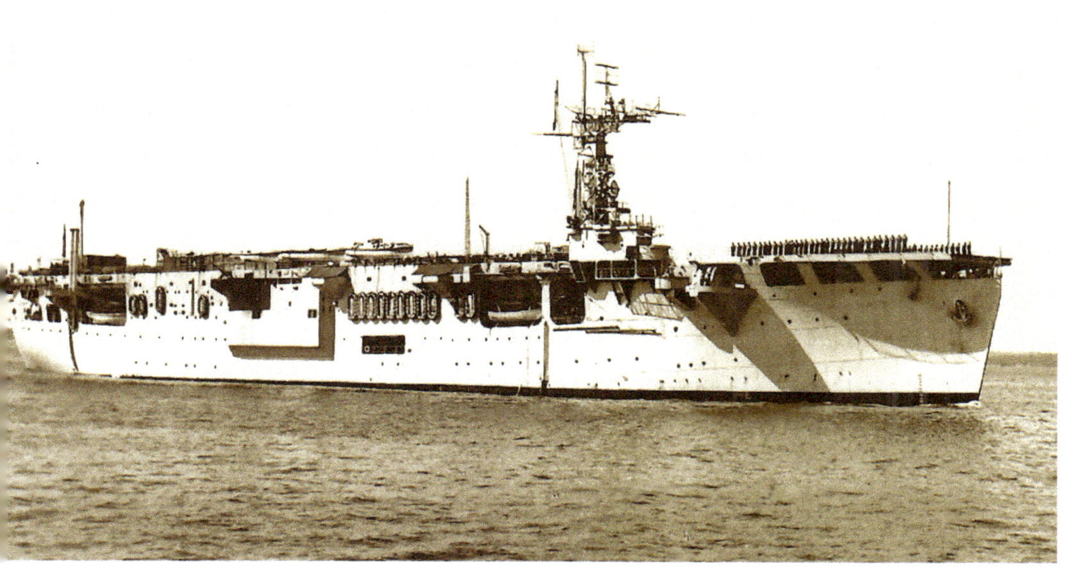

HMS *Campania.*

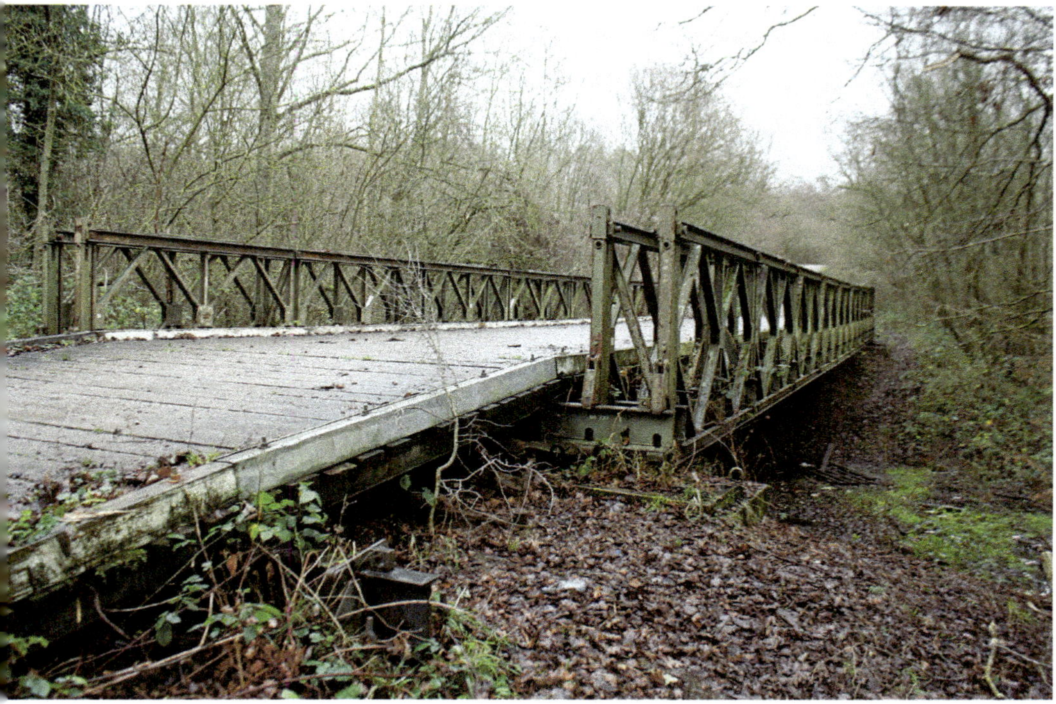

A Bailey Bridge at the Royal Engineers training area at Chattenden.

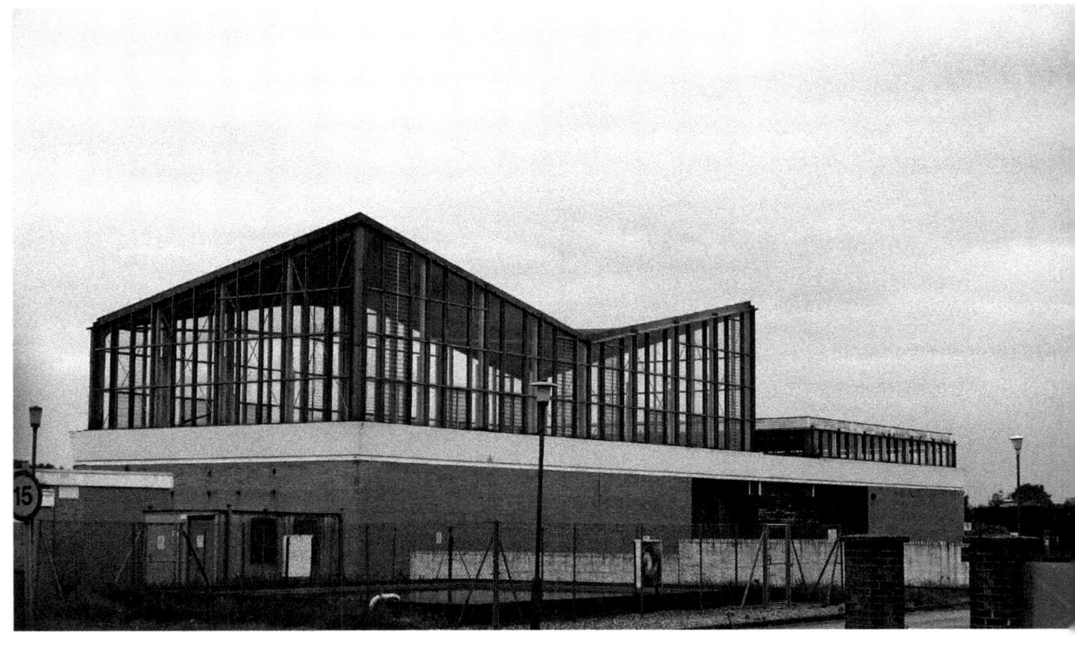

The Exhibition Hall at Lodge Hill Camp in 2017.

The Defence White Paper of 1957 instigated a further decline of the Royal Navy's activities on the Medway. The Nore Command, with its Chatham headquarters, was abolished; Sheerness Dockyard, the armaments depots at Lodge Hill and Upnor and the fuel depot on the Isle of Grain were closed. Doubts were soon being expressed about the future of the dockyard, but these were allayed when orders were received for the construction of the new *Oberon* class of submarines, the first of which, HMS *Oberon*, was laid down on No. 7 Slip in November 1957 and finally completed in February 1961.

A total of six of the class were built at Chatham, including three for the Royal Canadian Navy. The last of these, HMCS *Okanagan*, was launched on 17 September 1966, an occasion that became a significant landmark in Chatham's history as the launching of the last ever warship built at the dockyard.

The advent of nuclear-powered submarines seemed to predict the death knell for Chatham Dockyard. Britain's first, HMS *Dreadnought*, had been built at a private yard, Vickers Armstrong in Barrow-in-Furness, and launched in 1963. Chatham did not possess the facilities to either build or refit these new types of submarines and there were too few contracts for the refitting of surface vessels to keep the yard viable long term. However, one positive spin-off of the nuclear programme for Chatham Dockyard was that it was chosen to convert the large depot ship HMS *Forth* into a support vessel for the new nuclear submarine fleet.

In 1965, the Admiralty was absorbed into the newly formed Ministry of Defence, which would henceforth be responsible for the administration of all three armed services. This brought with it the total reorganisation of the management structure at the dockyard and fears of more job reductions. However, later in 1965 the government

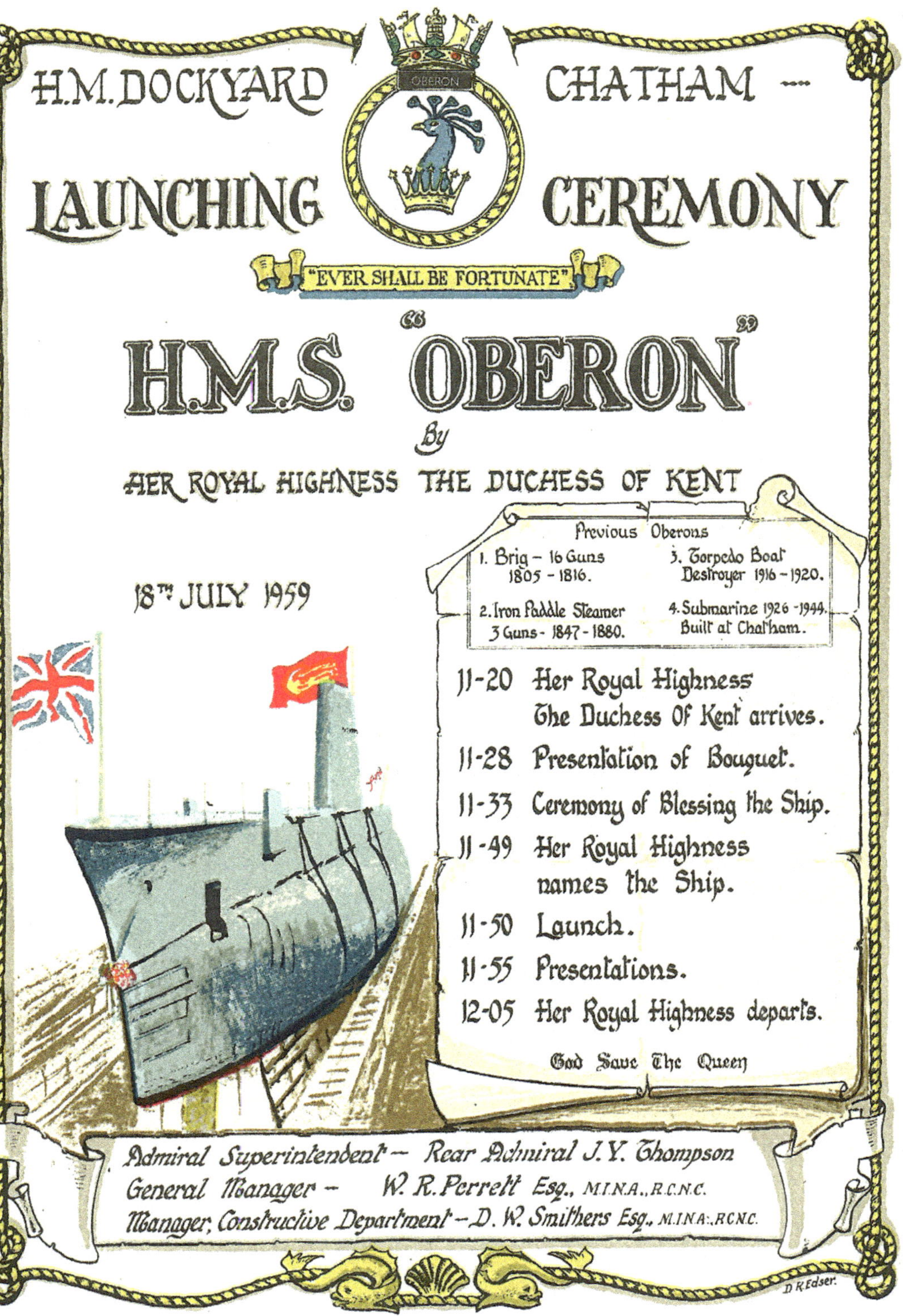

The launching ceremony programme for HMS *Oberon*.

H.M. DOCKYARD, CHATHAM

ADMIT BEARER

to view the Launch of

H.M.C.S. OKANAGAN

Saturday, 17th September, 1966

Please have this ticket
ready to show at the
Dockyard Gate

The colour of this tick
is the colour of yo
ENCLOSURE

Please read the instructions on the back of this ticket

Admittance ticket for the launch of HMCS *Okanagan*.

announced that a new nuclear refitting and refuelling complex was to be built at Chatham, which seemed to offer a bright new future for the dockyard. Despite local concerns about radiation safety, building approval was soon granted and work commenced on the construction of the complex, which was to be sited between No. 6 and No. 7 Docks in No. 1 Basin and would allow for two submarines to be worked on simultaneously.

The complex was completed in 1968, creating many new specialist jobs for the yard. The site was dominated by a huge 1,700-ton hammerhead crane, standing over 160 feet high, which was used for lifting the nuclear reactors and other heavy equipment in and out of the submarines. The crane's operator probably enjoyed the best view of the dockyard but had a long climb to get to it, and to save him climbing up and down during his working day some basic living quarters were incorporated within the crane's structure with toilet, washing and cooking facilities. The complex was opened by the Controller of the Navy, Vice-Admiral Horace Law, on 29 June 1968.

The first submarine to use the complex was HMS *Valiant*, which entered No. 6 Dock in May 1970 and was returned to the fleet two years later. In that time, she had been refuelled and completely refitted.

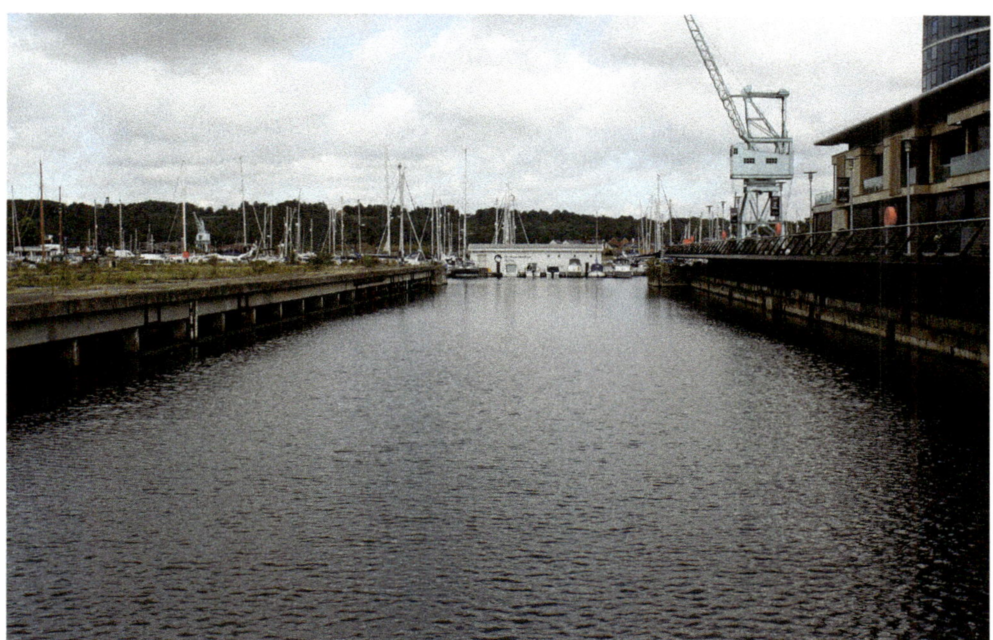

Above: No. 6 Dock in 2014.

Below: The hammerhead crane at the dockyard Nuclear Refit Complex *c.* 1975.

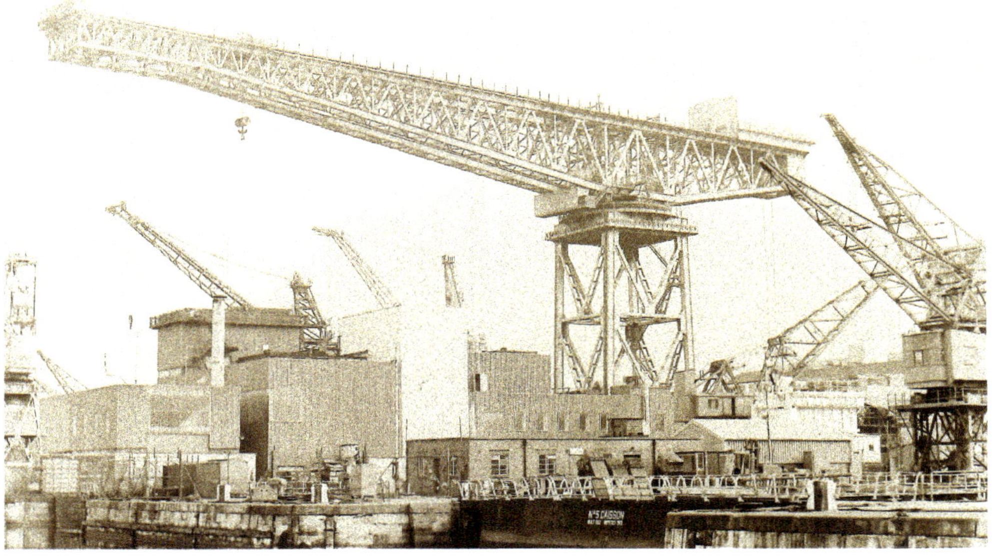

In 1971, further defence cuts saw Chatham's remaining naval establishments amalgamated into a single administrative entity as HM Naval Base, Chatham. Another consequence of the cuts saw the withdrawal of British forces from their bases 'East of Suez', which included the Far East Fleet from Singapore. Many ships were sold

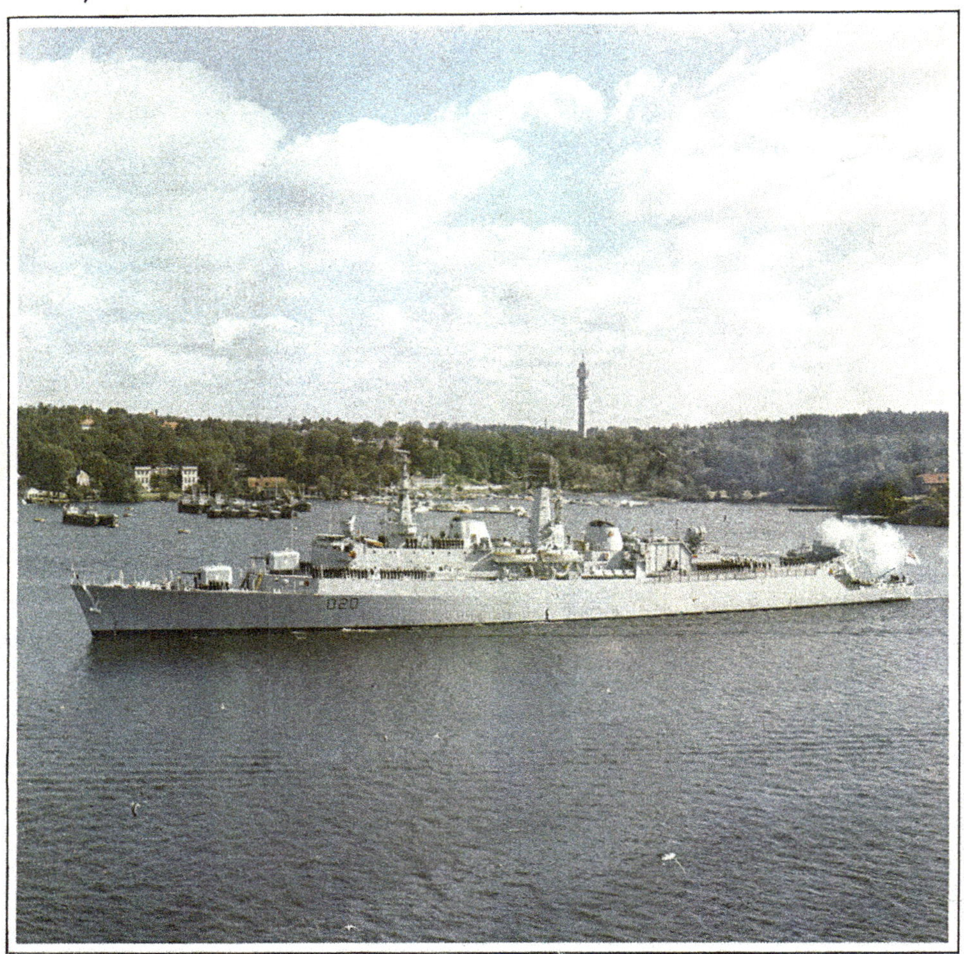

1975 Royal Navy Open Days programme.

or scrapped while others were laid up in reserve, one of which was the Heavy Repair Ship HMS *Triumph*, a converted Second World War era aircraft carrier. She paid off at Chatham in 1972 and was laid up in No. 3 Basin where she stayed for almost nine years, becoming a familiar sight for the thousands of visitors that continued to flock to the yard every May for the ever-popular 'Navy Days'.

Throughout the 1970s the dockyard continued with its nuclear submarine programme while continuing to be engaged with the refitting and repairing of some smaller surface ships. It was also still home to elements of the Reserve Fleet including the Frigate Standby Squadron. For a while it seemed that the yard had a bright future but, despite this new hope, on 25 June 1981, the Secretary of State for Defence, John Nott, announced in the House of Commons that the Chatham Navy Base was to close by 31 March 1984.

News of the base's closure came as a great shock to the people of the Medway Towns, especially with some redundancies being announced almost immediately. Protests and lobbies of parliament were organised, but nothing was going to change the government's mind. The fleet had been reduced to such a level that it could no longer sustain work at the four royal dockyards still in service. One had to go, and Chatham was the obvious choice, the other three, Portsmouth, Devonport and Rosyth, all having external commitments outside their immediate areas such as shore establishments and berthing facilities, which Chatham lacked.

Hopes of a reprieve came in April 1982 when Argentina invaded the Falkland Islands. The government quickly ordered that a large naval task force be dispatched with orders to retake the islands. All the royal dockyards were suddenly thrust into 'top gear' to prepare the task force. These included Chatham, where redundancy notices were suspended to ensure that maximum effort could be directed at the work. Structural alterations were made to a number of ships and urgently required stores and fuel were issued from the dockyard's stocks. With so many vessels heading for the South Atlantic and the Cold War still at its height, the Royal Navy's severely reduced presence in the North Atlantic and home waters became another serious concern. Orders were therefore issued to reactivate the Standby Squadron based at Chatham. This squadron was comprised of six 1960s vintage 'Tribal' class frigates, three of which had already been placed on the Disposal List. In the event only three of the ships would be returned to active service, replacing losses suffered in the South Atlantic, and this feat had only been made possible by stripping the other three vessels of vital parts that were no longer available from stores.

The end of the Falklands War saw crowds flock to the banks of the Medway to welcome home the Chatham-based Ice Patrol Ship HMS *Endurance* when she returned from the conflict on 20 August 1982. The vessel, with her small detachment of Royal Marine Commandos, had played a pivotal role in the initial stages of the war when she engaged Argentine forces landing on South Georgia with missiles from her Wasp helicopter, disabling an enemy submarine.

Unfortunately, there was to be no reprieve for Chatham. Redundancy notices were reinstated and more issued. On 3 June 1983, the Royal Naval Barracks HMS *Pembroke* held its final ceremonial divisions. On 29 October its last commanding officer, Captain Paddy Sheehan, was ceremonially 'hauled out' of the main gate by some of his men, leaving the barracks in the care of the Closure Party.

Meanwhile, in May 1983 HMS *Churchill* completed the last of the nine major submarine refit and refuelling's that had been carried out at the dockyard's Nuclear Complex and on 21 June the final Royal Navy vessel to be refitted at Chatham Dockyard, the frigate HMS *Hermione*, sailed out of the yard's Bulls Nose Locks. On 30 September the dockyard's closure was marked with an emotional Haul Down Ceremony in front of hundreds of dockyard workers and various dignitaries, as well as press and television from all over the world.

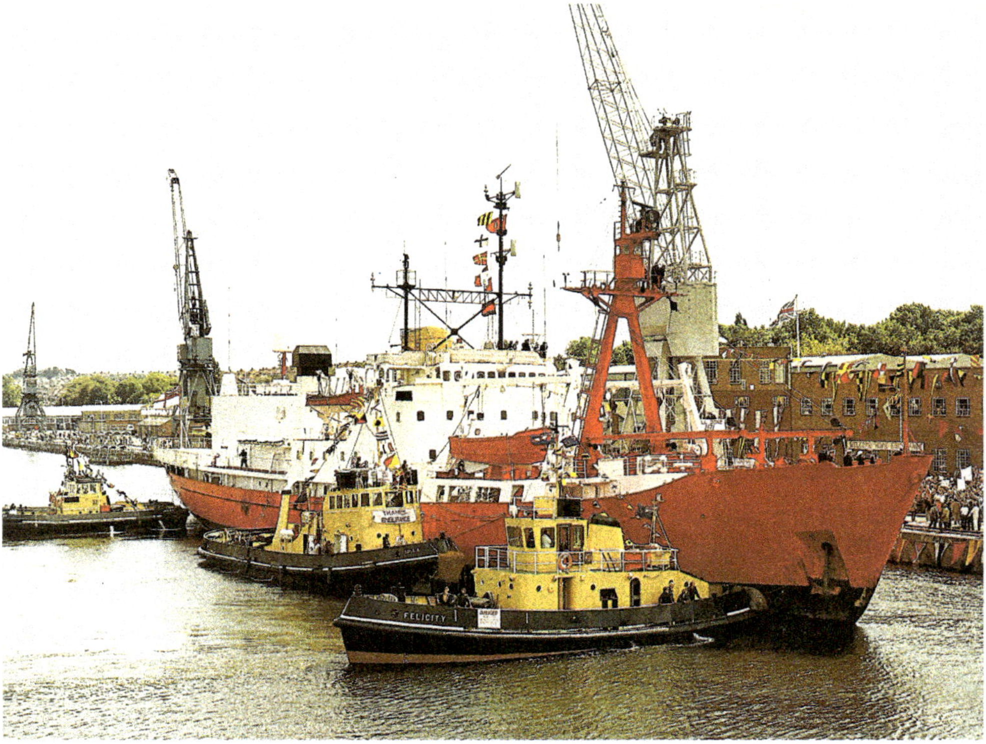

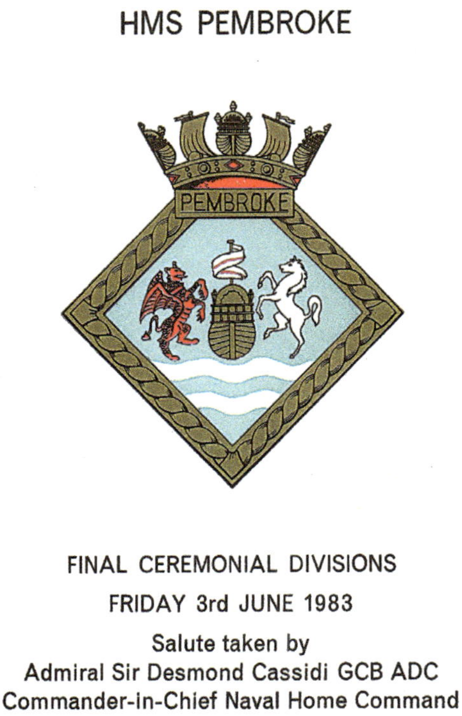

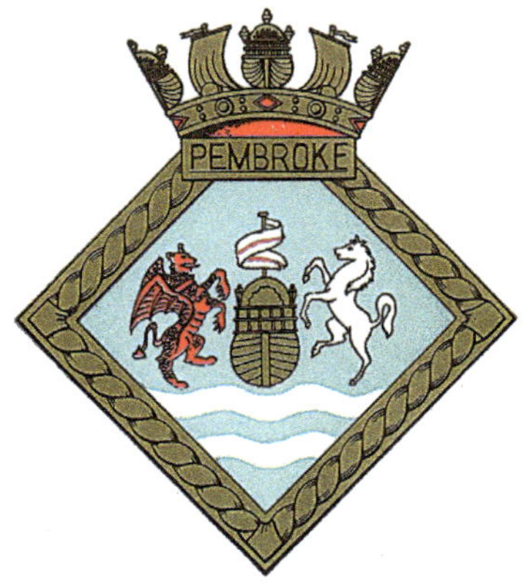

HMS PEMBROKE

Above: HMS *Endurance* on her return to Chatham from the Falklands conflict.

Left: The programme for Royal Navy Barracks Final Ceremonial Divisions.

FINAL CEREMONIAL DIVISIONS

FRIDAY 3rd JUNE 1983

Salute taken by
Admiral Sir Desmond Cassidi GCB ADC
Commander-in-Chief Naval Home Command

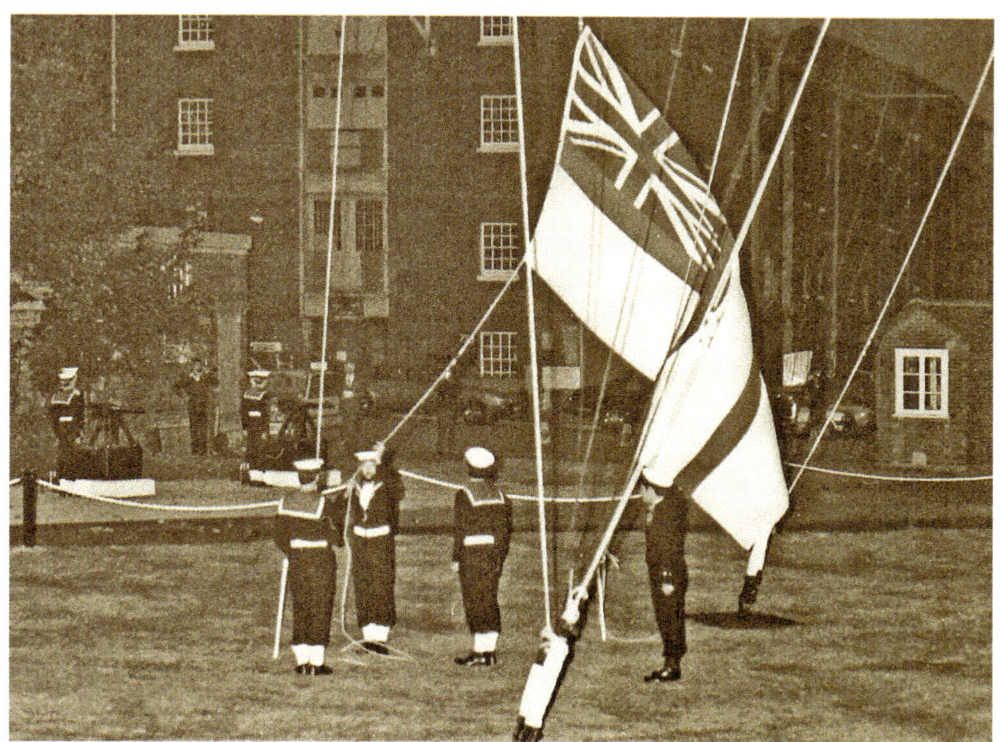

The White Ensign is hauled down for the last time at the dockyard.

On 18 February 1984 the small RN Closure Party gathered at the mast outside the wardroom at the naval barracks. The 'Last Post' was sounded by a solitary Royal Marines bugler and the White Ensign was lowered. The party left in a horse-drawn brewer's dray cart and the gates of HMS *Pembroke* were finally locked. Within a month Chatham Royal Dockyard was completely vacated and the Ministry of Defence police locked its gates for the last time on 31 March 1984, thus ending Chatham's 450-year association with the Royal Navy.

After the Royal Navy's withdrawal Chatham's military significance was severely reduced. The army's presence continued into the twenty-first century in the form of the Royal Engineers and the RSME with their training sites at Lodge Hill and Chattenden, but further cuts in the strength of the army had already begun to affect the Chatham Garrison before then with Chattenden Barracks being vacated by 12 RSME Regiment in 1995 and subsequently demolished. By the early 2000s the training sites were already being earmarked for possible future redevelopment and when the DEODS moved to Bicester in 2013, leaving Lodge Hill Camp redundant, their fate also seemed to be sealed. Around the same time the former RN Ordnance Depot at Lower Upnor, which had been used by the M.O.D. as stores since the 1960s, was put up for sale and another historic site, Kitchener Barracks, was vacated by the Royal Engineers and the site sold for redevelopment. The training sites at Lodge Hill and Chattenden were abandoned and eventually put up for sale in 2016.

Today the military presence in Chatham is but a shadow of its former self. The garrison is concentrated on the Royal Engineers Brompton Barracks and the RSME, which also still maintains a small presence across the river at Upper Upnor at its Riverine Operations Section, which specialises in the training of Assault Boat Operators and Watermanship Safety Officers. Many of the old military sites have disappeared through redevelopment or been converted into housing. Much of the fortifications of the Chatham Lines can still be seen and Fort Amherst is a major tourist attraction.

Following the Royal Navy's departure from Chatham in 1984 the old Georgian era Royal Dockyard was taken over by the Chatham Historic Dockyard Trust and has become one of Kent's top tourist attractions. Some of the preserved buildings have been let to the University of Kent for tuition space or to private companies for commercial purposes. The Victorian dockyard on St Mary's Island has almost completely disappeared under housing and a large retail outlet centre, although the three giant basins remain with No. 3 Basin being operated as the commercial Chatham Docks and No. 1 Basin as a public marina. The former Royal Naval Barracks, HMS *Pembroke*, is now a campus of the University of Greenwich, which attracts thousands of students from around the world to study within its historic walls.

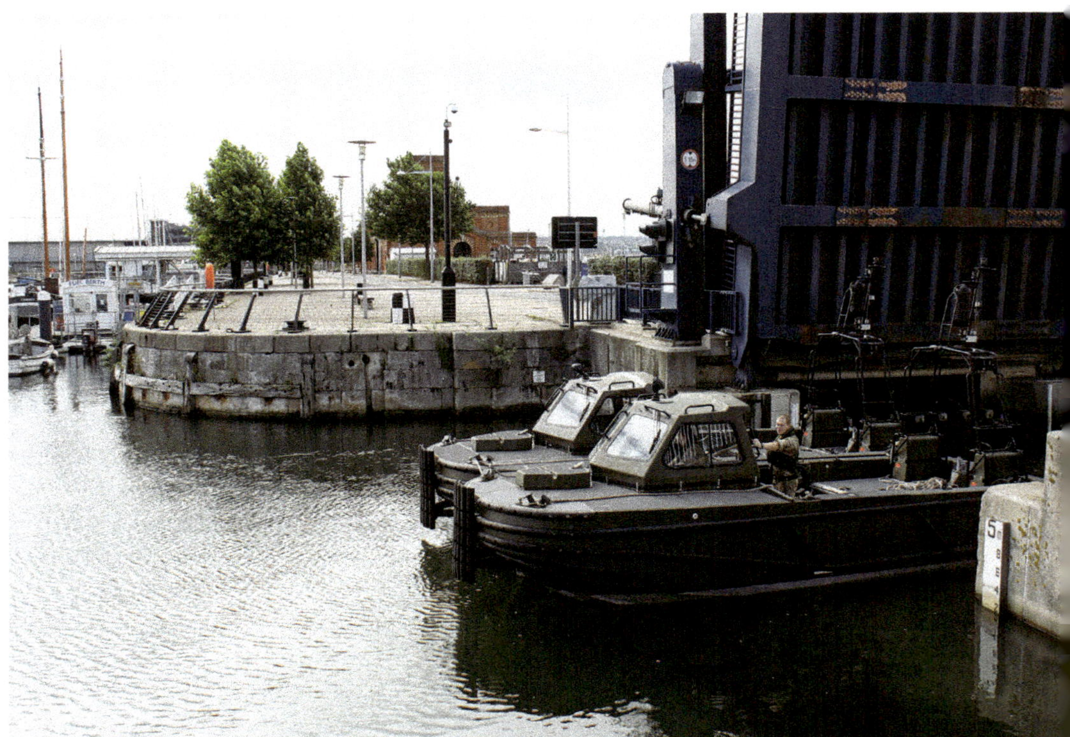

Royal Engineers assault boats entering No. 1 Basin to refuel in 2014.

7. Personalities

Among those living on the hulks laid up on the Medway in the mid-sixteenth century was a family from Tavistock in Devon. The father was a Protestant preacher, the Revd Edmund Drake. He'd been forced to flee the West Country when the local population, who were mostly Catholics, turned on him when the new Book of Common Prayer was introduced into church services in 1549. Edmund decided to flee with his family to Portsmouth where he found service as a preacher on board one of His Majesty's ships. In 1550, it was ordered that all the 'Kinges shippes should be harborowed in Gillingham Waters' and so the vessels at Portsmouth were transferred to the Medway. Edmund and his large family were housed on one of the old hulks and he was charged with the duty of preaching to all the seamen posted to Chatham. In 1560, Edmund was appointed vicar of Upnor but continued to live with his family on the hulks. One of Edmund's sons was none other than Francis (later Sir Francis) Drake, who became famous as the admiral who defeated the Spanish Armada. Francis was a boy of aroud six years old when he came with his family to live on the Medway. His early youth was spent on the river watching the ships of the navy come and go and listening to tales of far-off lands from the retired seamen who acted as watchmen on the hulks. He would have watched the seamen at work on the ships and

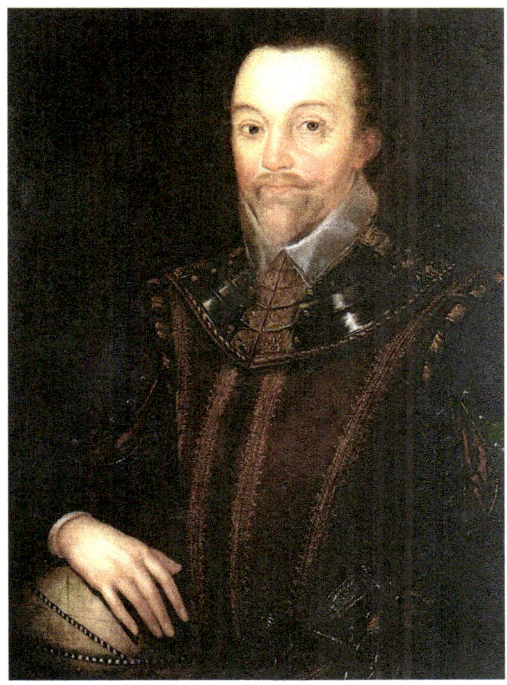

Sir Francis Drake.

learnt from them the ways of the sea and the sailor. It's fair to say that one of England's greatest admirals found the inspiration for his illustrious future career at Chatham.

A naval contemporary and second cousin of Drake's, also with strong ties to Chatham, was Sir John Hawkins. Born into a family of wealthy Devonshire merchants, Hawkins made his fortune from the slave trade and privateering.

Hawkins was appointed Treasurer of the Admiralty in 1578. It was while serving in this office that he first became associated with Chatham. A major duty of his office was to keep the Queen's Navy in good repair and in doing so he worked closely with the Elizabethan dockyard's two Master Shipwrights, Matthew Baker and Peter Pett. Hawkins also concerned himself with the defences of the dockyard. Fearing a Spanish raid on the Medway, he ordered that a substantial chain be stretched across the river from Upnor to St Mary's Creek to prevent Spanish ships reaching Chatham and burning the English vessels anchored there.

He also became heavily involved with the navy's shipbuilding and it was his small, fast and heavily gunned design of warship that was instrumental in defeating the Spanish Armada, in which battle he himself served as a Rear Admiral and one of the three commanders of the English fleet along with Drake and Frobisher.

In 1589, concerned with the fate of seamen wounded in the Armada battle, Hawkins, in conjunction with Drake, founded the 'Chatham Chest' – a pension fund for disabled sailors. It was financed by regular contributions from seamen's wages and the money kept in a chest in Chatham Dockyard. Hawkins also founded a hospital and almshouse for aged and infirm seamen in Chatham, which still exists today. The Hospital of Sir John Hawkins is now the world's oldest surviving naval charity.

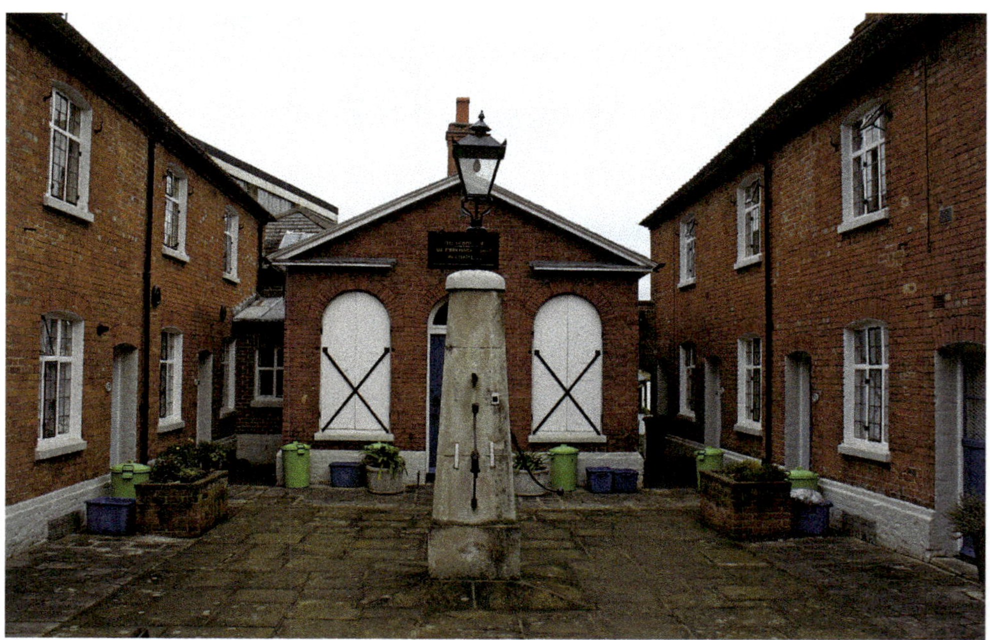

The Hospital of Sir John Hawkins in the High Street, Chatham.

Another famous mariner with a Chatham connection is Robert Barlow. He was born in Covent Garden, London, on Christmas Day 1757. He joined the navy at an early age and married in 1785. He was promoted to Lieutenant of HMS *Courageux* and participated in the capture of the French frigate *Minerve* in 1781. In 1794, he commanded HMS *Pegasus* at Lord Howe's victory over the French fleet. He was subsequently appointed to the command of HMS *Phoebe*, and after a severe battle he captured the French frigate *Néréide*. In 1801 he succeeded in capturing *L'africane*, laden with military supplies and 400 French troops, which had been destined to join the French army in Egypt. Barlow was subsequently knighted and appointed to the seventy-four-gun HMS *Triumph*. In 1806, he was appointed Deputy-Controller of the Navy, and then made Commissioner of Chatham Dockyard in 1808, an office he occupied until 1823. He was appointed a Knight-Commander of the Most Honourable Order of the Bath in 1820. Barlow resigned in 1823, with the rank of retired Admiral, but in 1840, at the age of eighty-three, he was recalled to active duty, and made Admiral of the White. He died on 11 May 1843 at the Archbishop's Palace at Canterbury, where he had been living for some years, and he was buried at Gillingham. His daughter, Hilaire, married Lord Nelson's eldest brother, William, first Earl Nelson in 1829.

Being a major garrison town for over 300 years, it is no surprise that Chatham has had many notable army officers associated with it over that time. One of the most important but probably among the least well known was Lieutenant-General Sir John Moore. Born in Glasgow in 1761, he left school at the age of eleven to join his father on the 'Grand Tour' when, for four years, he travelled around Europe before becoming an Ensign in

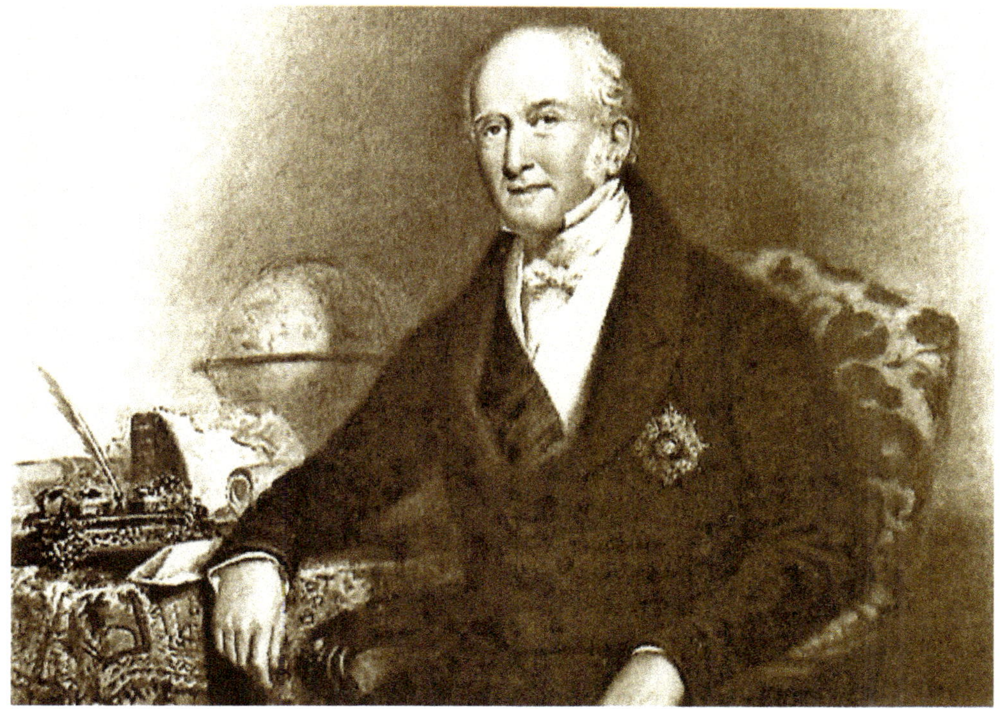

Admiral Sir Robert Barlow.

the 51st Regiment of Foot. He distinguished himself in battle during the American War of Independence, as a result of which he was promoted to Captain. Moore first came to Chatham in 1788 where he was brought into the new 4th battalion of the 60th Royal Rifles for a short time before transferring back to his old regiment, the 51st. He went on to serve in campaigns in Corsica, the West Indies and the Mediterranean.

His campaign experience had given him some very definite ideas regarding infantry tactics and training. He had been impressed with the skirmishing tactics of the various French light infantry units he had encountered and was convinced that similar tactics should be adopted into the British Army. He became Colonel of the 52nd Regiment of Foot in 1801 and when they were stationed at Chatham in 1802, he began training them in light infantry tactics before they moved to Shorncliffe in 1803 where they joined a brigade, which Moore was to command. The brigade was formed to meet the threat of French invasion and, now a Major-General, Moore was put in charge of the defence of the coast between Dover and Dungeness. In this capacity he was instrumental in the building of the chain of Martello Tower forts along the coast as well as the Royal Military Canal.

Moore died at the Battle of Corunna in 1809, but not before his light infantry training methods and tactics had been adopted into many British regiments, contributing considerably to Wellington's later victories in Spain and at Waterloo.

Charles William Pasley was born at Eskdale Muir, Dumfriesshire, Scotland in 1780. He was highly intelligent, capable of translating the New Testament from Greek at the age of eight. The general was educated for the Royal Artillery, and in that branch of the army obtained his commission as second lieutenant in December 1797, but he was transferred to the Royal Engineers the following year. He distinguished himself in combat in several battles during the Napoleonic Wars, serving under Lieutenant-General Sir John Moore

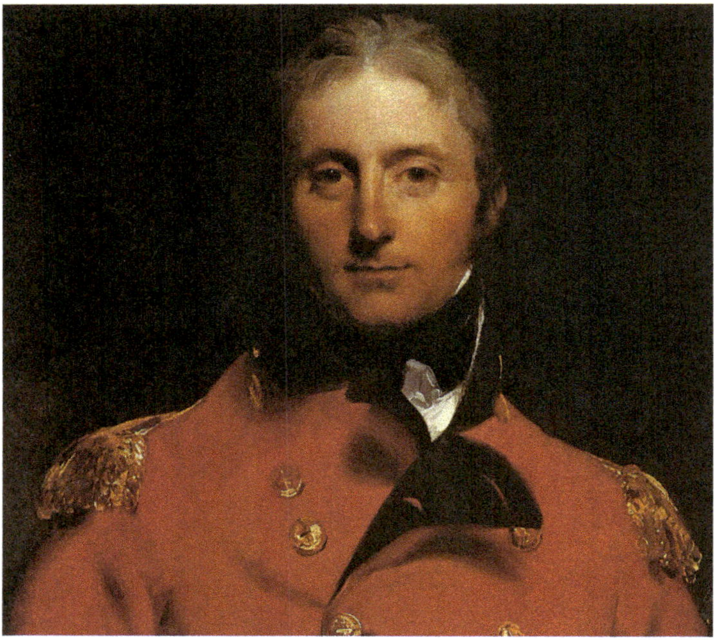

Lieutenant-General
Sir John Moore.

CHIEFLY DEDUCED FROM EXPERIMENT,

FOR CONDUCTING THE

PRACTICAL OPERATIONS OF A SIEGE,

BY

C. W. PASLEY, LIEUT.-COL. R.E., F.R.S. &c.

PART I.

CONTAINING THE PREPARATION OF THE NECESSARY MATERIALS, AND THE TRACING AND EXECUTION OF THE FIRST AND SECOND PARALLELS, AND OF THE APPROACHES CONNECTED WITH THEM.

PRINTED

FOR THE USE OF THE ESTABLISHMENT FOR FIELD INSTRUCTION

CHATHAM.

1829

A manual on siege operations written by Lieutenant-Colonel C. W. Pasley in 1829.

at the Battle of Corunna. He was appointed the first Director of Field Instruction at the newly formed Royal Engineers Establishment, which later became the School of Military Engineering, at Brompton Barracks in 1812, a position he held until 1841 when he was promoted to the rank of Major-General. While at Chatham, in 1838, he was presented with the freedom of the City of London for his services in removing sunken vessels from the bed of the Thames near Gravesend. He then undertook the task of blowing up the wreck of the *Royal George* at Spithead in 1839–41, superintending all the operations. On being relieved of his duties at Chatham, he was appointed Inspector-General of Railways in the Board of Trade.

Probably the greatest maverick among the army officers that passed through Chatham was Major-General Charles Gordon. Born in 1833 into an old established military family, he was educated at Taunton School and the Royal Military Academy in Woolwich. He was commissioned into the Royal Engineers as a Second-Lieutenant in 1852. He spent two years at Chatham completing his training before being promoted to full Lieutenant in 1854. At the age of twenty-one he had already gained a reputation for disregarding authority and flouting the rules, but as a young officer he also showed charisma and strong leadership qualities.

He served in the Crimean War with some distinction, particularly at the Siege of Sebastopol where he was wounded while mapping out the Russian fortifications. After the war he was sent to delineate the frontier between Russian and Turkish Armenia. To aid in this task he used the new media of photography and he was elected a fellow of the Royal Geographical Society for his collection of photographs of Armenia.

He returned to Chatham in 1858 where he was appointed as an instructor and then promoted to Captain in 1859.

In 1860, he volunteered to serve in China where a small British force was assisting the Imperial Chinese Army fighting Taiping rebels. Gordon ended up commanding the Chinese force in Sonjiang Province, which became known as the 'Ever Victorious Army' for winning a string of victories. Gordon himself became known as 'Chinese Gordon' and was often photographed dressed in Chinese robes.

Gordon returned to Britain and was stationed at Gravesend where he directed the Royal Engineers in building forts to defend the Thames Estuary, a task he regarded as 'expensive and useless'.

In 1872, Gordon was serving in Egypt, then still nominally part of the Ottoman Empire, when he was approached by the Ottoman Khedive to serve as Governor of Equatoria Province (modern-day South Sudan). The British government agreed, and he was such a success that he was later appointed as Governor-General of the entire Sudan, based at its capital, Khartoum. It was here in 1885 that Gordon met his fate when the city was besieged by forces of the Mahdi who had rebelled against Egyptian rule. The rebels eventually broke through the city's defences and Gordon was killed on the steps of the Governor-General's palace.

The Royal Engineers at Chatham can also boast a royal family connection: Prince Arthur was the third son of Queen Victoria. Born in 1850, he joined the Royal Military Academy at Woolwich in 1866 from where he was commissioned into the Royal Engineers at Chatham in 1868. A report in the *Glasgow Herald* from 25 June 1868 records the event:

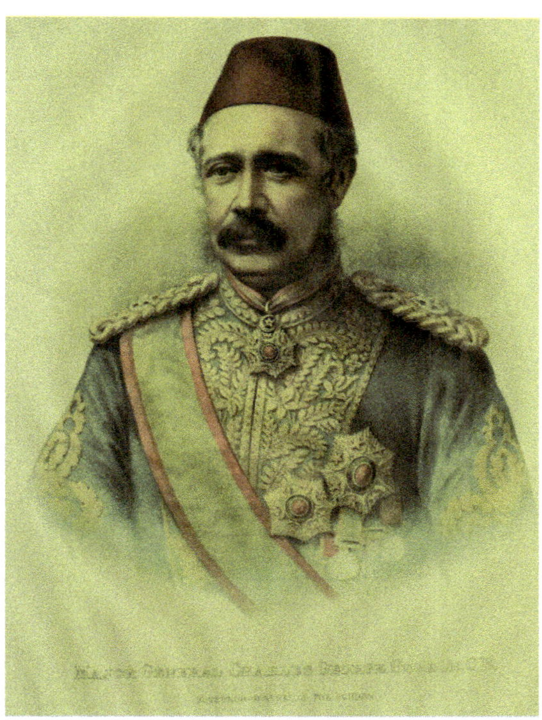

General Charles Gordon.

> Prince Arthur joined the Royal Engineer establishment at Chatham yesterday, for the purpose of commencing his studies with the corps of the Royal Engineers, in which he has just received a commission. The Captain-Superintendents House, in Chatham Dockyard, occupied by the superintendent of that establishment, has been set apart for his residence, a separate entrance having been erected at the dockyard for the use of the Prince in passing to and from the yard to Brompton Barracks. His Royal Highness, while stationed at Chatham will go through the usual curriculum of study in military engineering, topography, fortification, and the other subjects to be acquired by officers of the Royal Engineers. A suite of rooms has been set apart for his use during the time he is at Brompton Barracks.

Prince Arthur's time in the Royal Engineers was short-lived as he transferred to the Royal Artillery on 2 November 1868. He went on to have a long military career and was made Field Marshall in 1902 and Inspector-General of the Forces in 1904.

He had been created Duke of Connaught and Strathearn in 1874 and was appointed Governor-General of Canada in 1911. He died at Bagshot Park in 1942. Prince Arthur Road in Brompton was named in his honour.

Probably the most iconic military figure to be associated with Chatham was Field Marshall Earl Kitchener of Khartoum. Herbert Kitchener was born in Ireland in 1850. He was educated in Switzerland and later at the Royal Military Academy, Woolwich. He was commissioned into the Royal Engineers in 1871 and spent two years at the School of Military Engineering at Brompton. In 1883, he was promoted to Captain and posted to Egypt, where he joined the failed expedition to relieve General Gordon, then under siege

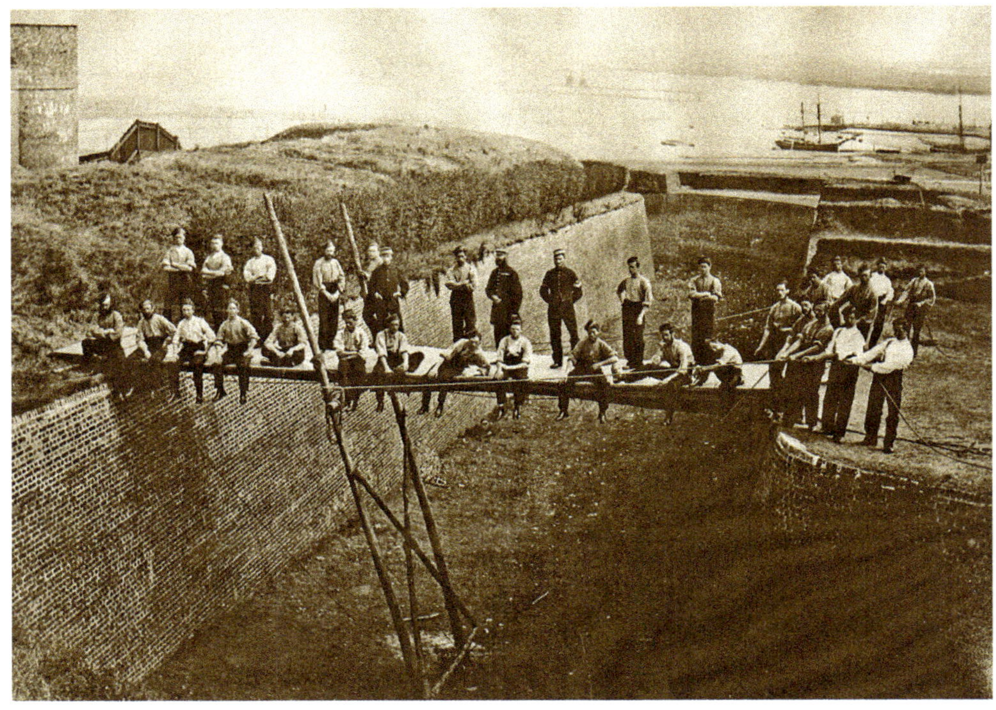

Prince Arthur (standing sixth from left) bridge building on the Lower Lines.

at Khartoum. In 1890, he was appointed Inspector-General of the Egyptian Police and then, in 1892, he was appointed Commander-in-Chief of the Egyptian Army. He led the reconquest of the Sudan from 1896–98.

In 1899, Kitchener arrived in South Africa as Second-in-Command of the British forces under Lord Roberts, who he succeeded as Commander-in-Chief in 1900. After the British victory in the Boer War he was promoted to full General and returned to Britain. On his return Edward VII invested him with the Order of Merit and created him Viscount Kitchener of Khartoum. He was then appointed Commander-in-Chief, India, and, in 1909, created a Field Marshall. He returned to Egypt in 1911 as British Consul-General and created Earl Kitchener in June 1914.

At the outbreak of the First World War he was recalled from Egypt and made Minister of War. His face became famous when it featured on the recruiting posters of the time with the words 'Your Country Needs You' emblazoned across them. The massive recruiting campaign was a huge success with millions signing up into 'Kitchener's New Army'.

He left Britain aboard the cruiser HMS *Hampshire* on 5 June 1916 on a mission to meet with Russian allies at Archangel. The vessel struck a German mine and sunk just west of the Orkney Islands. Kitchener went down with the ship and his body was never recovered.

When the Royal Engineers took over Chatham Barracks from the infantry in the 1920s they renamed them Kitchener Barracks in his honour, and, in 1960 after Sudan's independence from Britain, a statue of him that had stood in Khartoum since 1920 was shipped to Britain and re-erected on Dock Road outside the Kitchener Barracks.

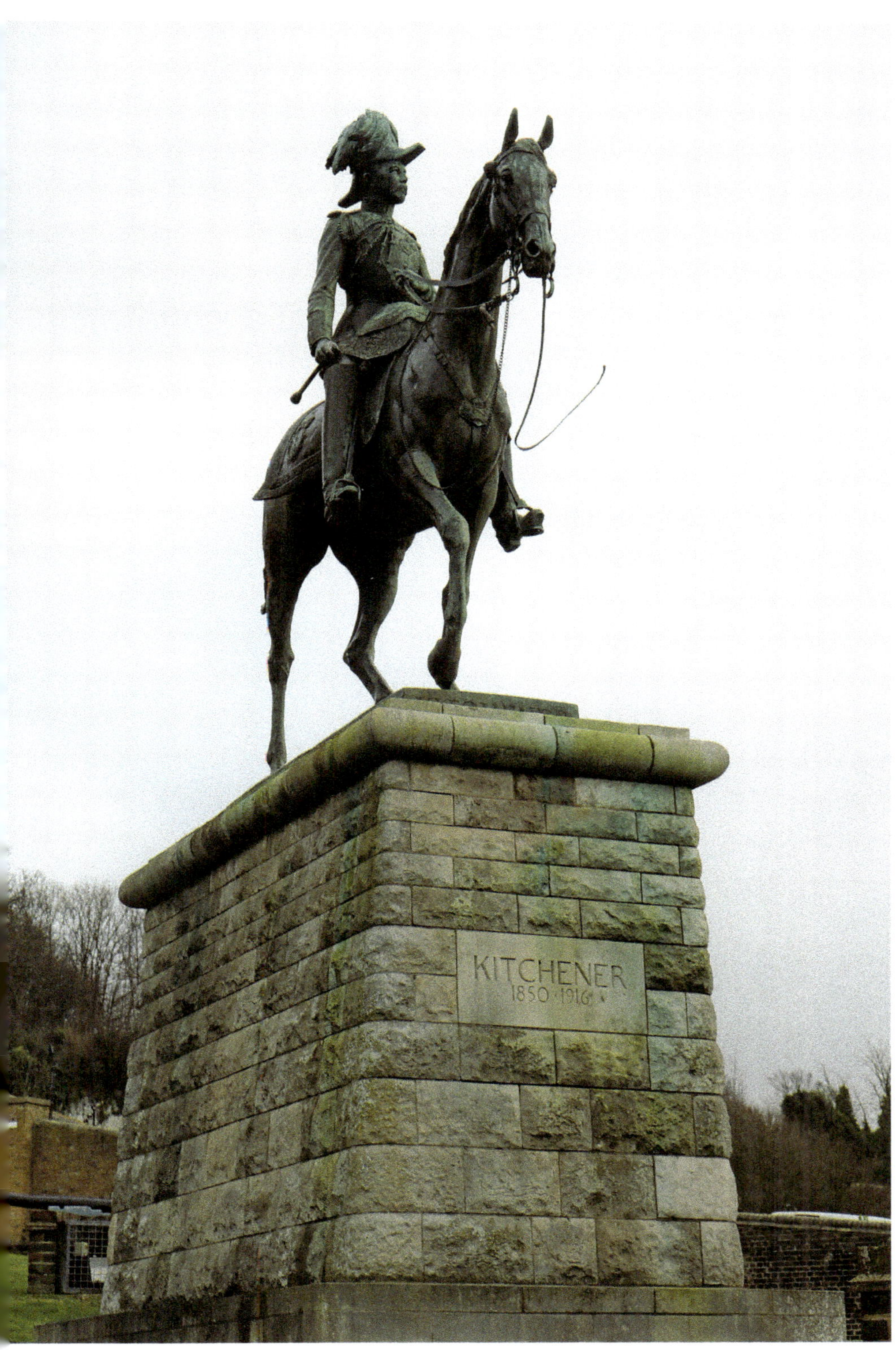

Lord Kitchener's statue on Dock Road.

James Michael 'Mike' Calvert was one of the most colourful and courageous British Army officers of the Second World War. He was born in India in 1913. His father was an English member of the Indian Civil Service. At the age of six his mother brought him back to England to begin his schooling. At the age of eighteen he joined the Royal Military Academy, Woolwich, as a cadet and in 1933 he was commissioned into the Royal Engineers and posted to the SME at Chatham.

After training at Chatham, he went up to Cambridge to read mechanical sciences and while there won a Blue for swimming. He also boxed for the army and became their middleweight champion.

In 1934, he was posted to the Hong Kong Royal Engineers, where he learned to speak Cantonese. After witnessing the Japanese attack on Shanghai, he became one of the few officers in the British Army convinced of the threat posed by Japanese imperialism.

Following the outbreak of the Second World War, Calvert saw service in Norway and trained commandos in demolition techniques in Hong Kong and Australia. In 1941, he was appointed to command the Bush Warfare School in Burma, training officers and NCOs to lead guerrilla bands in China for operations against the Japanese.

In 1943, he led one of General Orde Wingate's famous Chindit columns in their first operations behind the Japanese lines in Burma. For his part in the operation he was awarded the DSO.

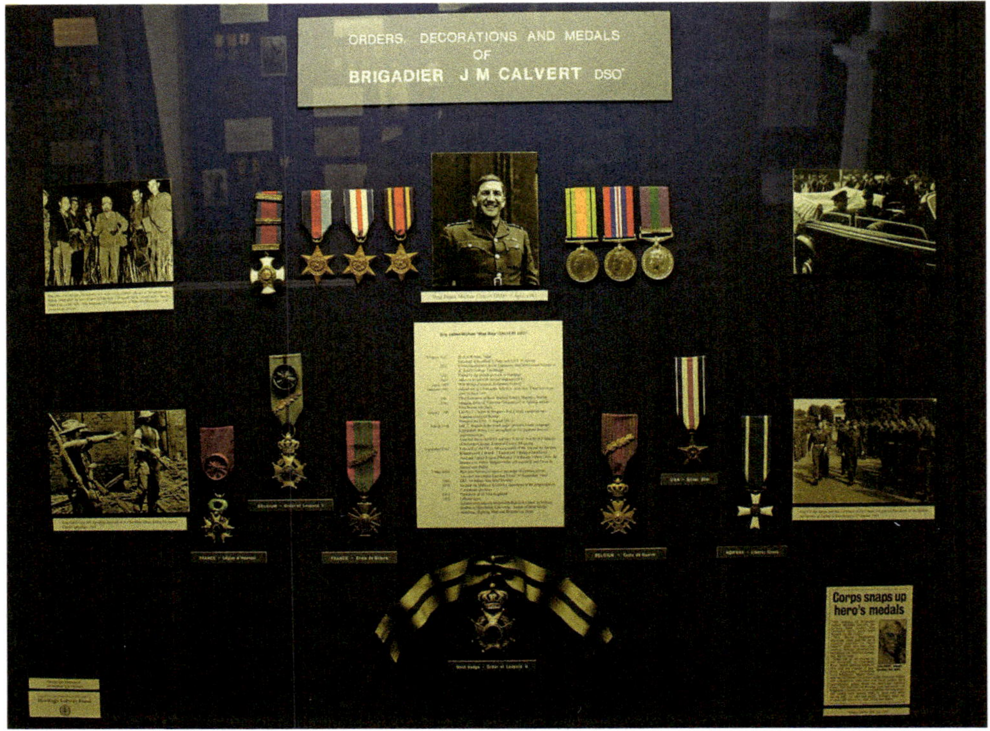

'Mike' Calvert's medals and decoration on display at the Royal Engineers Museum, Brompton.

In 1944, he commanded the 77th Indian Infantry Brigade in 'Operation Thursday', the second and much larger Chindit expedition with his brigade spearheading the airborne glider landings deep behind enemy lines.

He returned to Britain in October 1944 and, in March 1945, was given command of the Special Air Service Brigade, an appointment he held until the brigade's disbandment in October 1945.

He was dismissed from the army following a scandal in 1952. He died in Richmond-on-Thames in 1998. His medals and decorations were purchased by the Royal Engineers Museum at Brompton, where they can be seen on display today.

8. Significant Buildings

Dockyard Commissioner's House

This grand residence was built in 1704 and is the oldest surviving naval building in England. Its first occupant was the Yard's Resident Commissioner, Captain George St. Lo. In later years it was the home of the Yard's Admiral Superintendent and then the Port Admiral and was known as Admiralty House and later, in the 1970s, as Medway House. Internally the centrepiece is a magnificent ceiling painting above the main staircase. Painted on wood panel and depicting a scene the Greek gods assembling, it is believed to have come from the Great Cabin of the *Royal Sovereign*, an important first-rate ship of the line, broken up at Chatham in 1768.The Commissioner's House now provides a popular venue for weddings and corporate events

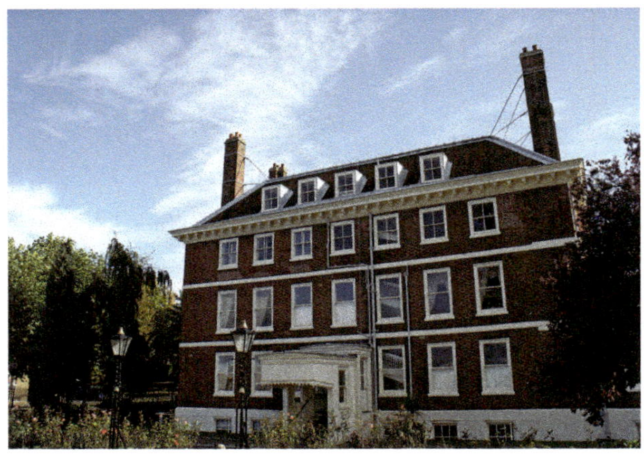

Dockyard Commissioner's House.

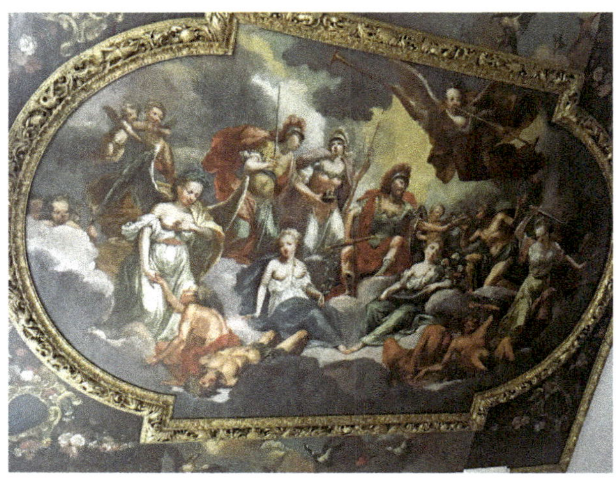

The ceiling painting above the
main staircase.

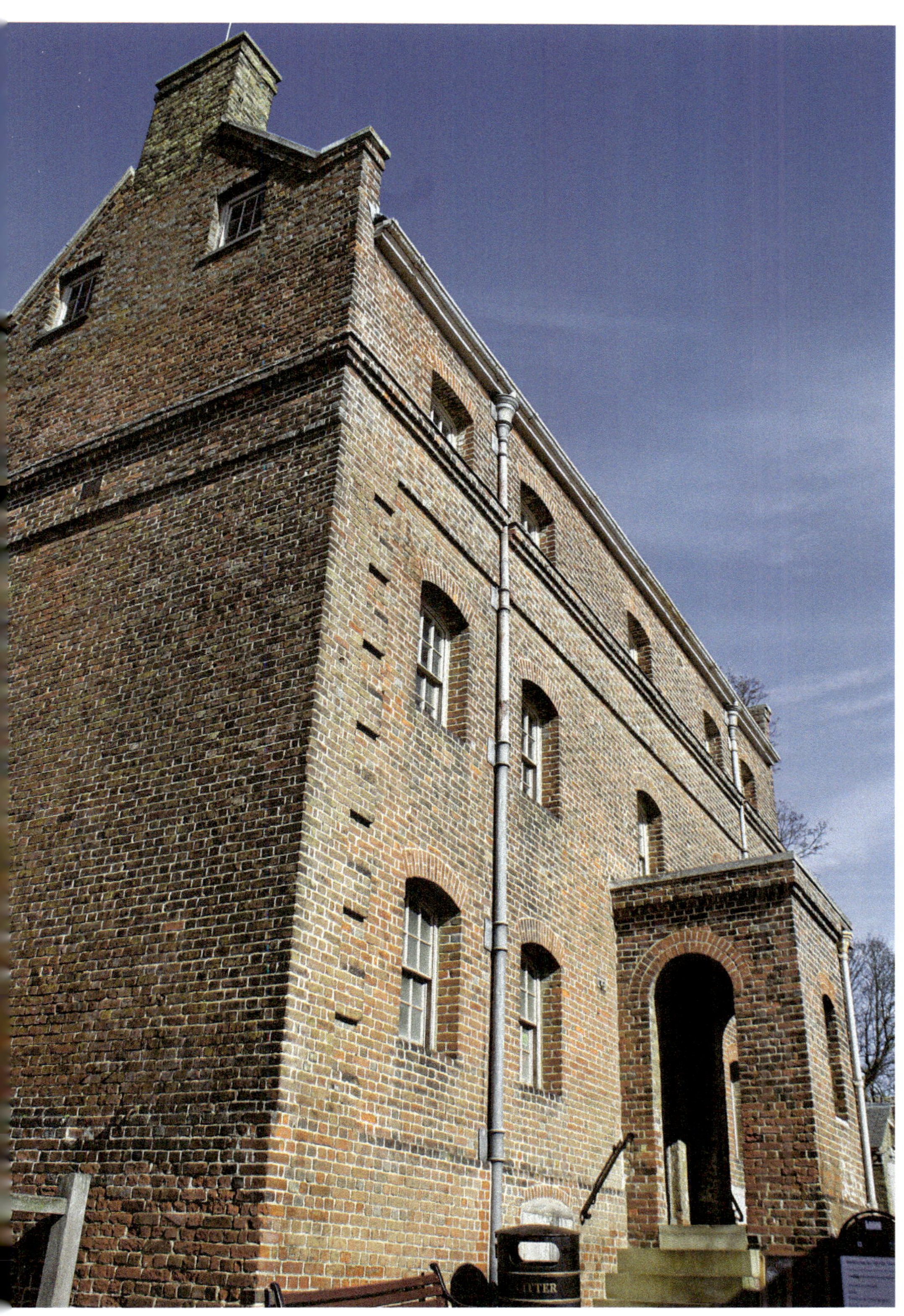

Upnor Castle Barracks.

Upnor Castle Barracks

When the Board of Ordnance took over the naval powder magazine at Upnor Castle they became seriously concerned about its security. Because of these concerns the board were prompted to establish a permanent military presence at the castle to guard the magazine, and to house them a new barracks was built to the south-west of the castle in 1719. The barracks were deigned to accommodate two officers and sixty-four men. They were the first purpose-built barracks provided at Chatham and the structure is now one of the oldest surviving barrack buildings in the UK.

Double Rope House, Chatham Dockyard

Rope has been made at Chatham Dockyard since 1618. It was made from raw hemp, which from the late eighteenth century was imported by ship from southern Russia and unloaded at the hemp houses at Chatham. In 1786, the Navy Board produced for the Admiralty plans for a new Rope Yard at Chatham. These consisted of a new Rigging and Storehouse, Hatchelling House, Yarn Stores, Tarring House and a double Rope House. The project was substantially complete by 1791. This Rope House is the most impressive of these new buildings. Its overall length is 1,140 feet with a width of 47 feet. The ground floor, known as the Rope Walk, was for laying ropes and cables and contained the bulk of the machinery. The forming machines travelled the whole length of the building pulled by huge winches. Each winch would be powered by fifty-nine men. In 1826, a steam engine

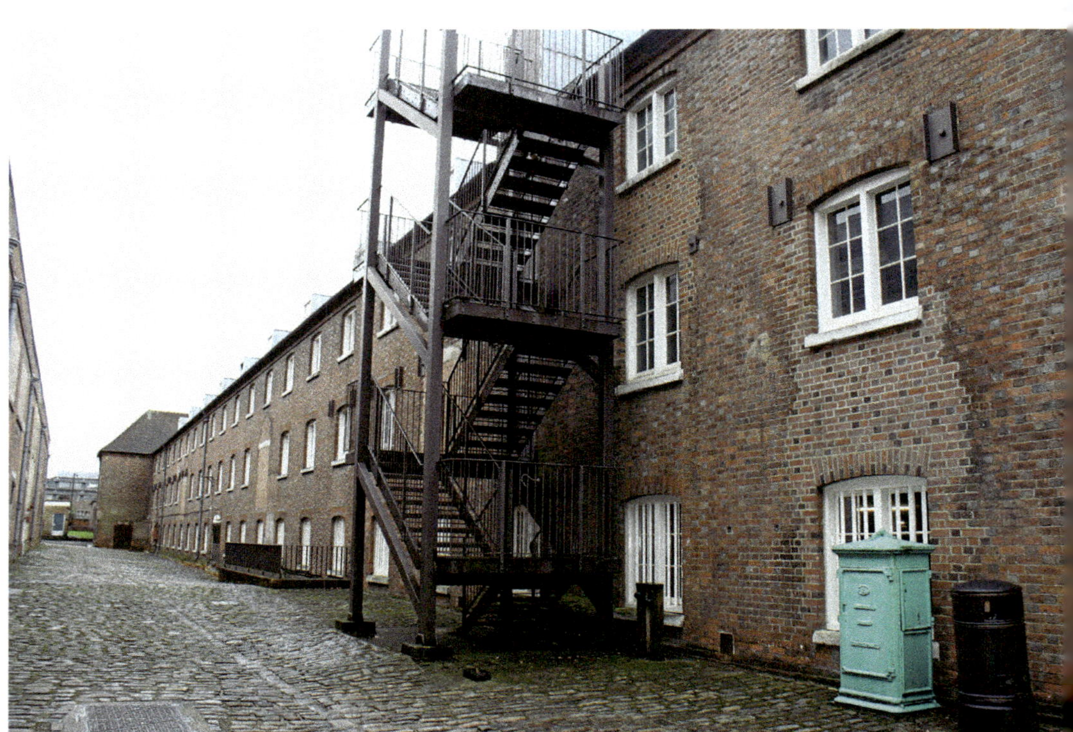

The Rope House looking south.

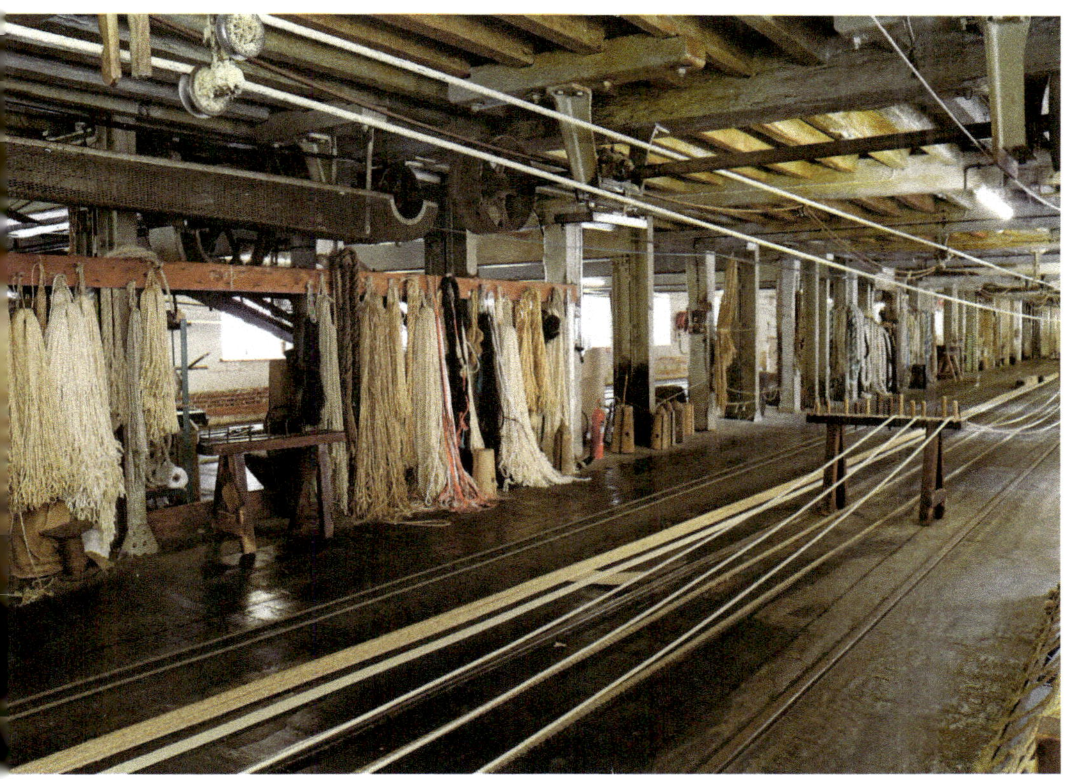

The Rope Walk.

was installed to drive the machinery, much of which survives and is still in use today. The completed rope was then used to form sets of rigging for each individual ship. These sets of rigging were hung and stored in the Rigging House. The Ropery now manufactures rope commercially using much of the original machinery and it is also one of the historic dockyard's main visitor attractions.

Sawmill, Chatham Dockyard

Designed by French-born engineer Marc Brunel (the father of Isambard Kingdom Brunel) and constructed 1812–14, the sawmill revolutionised the movement and storage of timber in the dockyard, which had previously employed over 900 sawyers to manually cut the timber and numerous teams of horses to transport it. The sawmill was powered by steam and connected by a canal and tunnel to the dockyard's south mast pond where the logs were stored and seasoned. The timber was lifted by a floating platform up a shaft. An overhead rail carried it to stores north of the mill, from where it could be retrieved in the same way. Logs were delivered to the mill and converted to planks by eight reciprocating cast-iron frames, which each carried an average of thirty-six saws, so producing 1,260 feet of sawing per minute. The mill's steam engine was also used to pump water around the dockyard. The building still operates as a sawmill today but little of the original machinery remains.

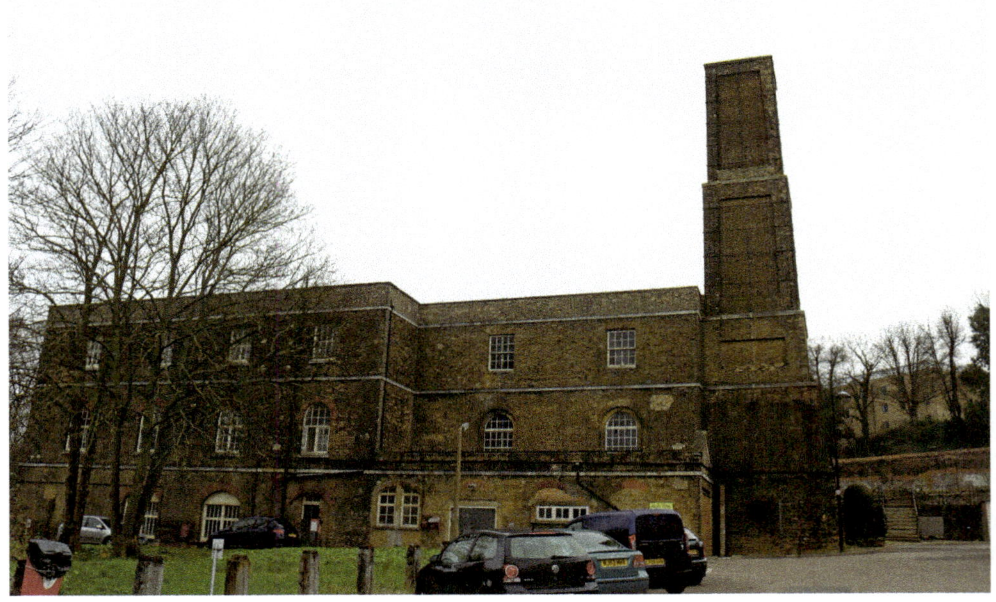

Brunel's Sawmill.

Chatham Garrison Gymnasium

The Garrison Gymnasium was built in 1863 on the orders of the Commander-in-Chief of the British Army at the time the Duke of Cambridge, who had been greatly concerned at the poor levels of physical fitness displayed by British troops during the Crimean War.

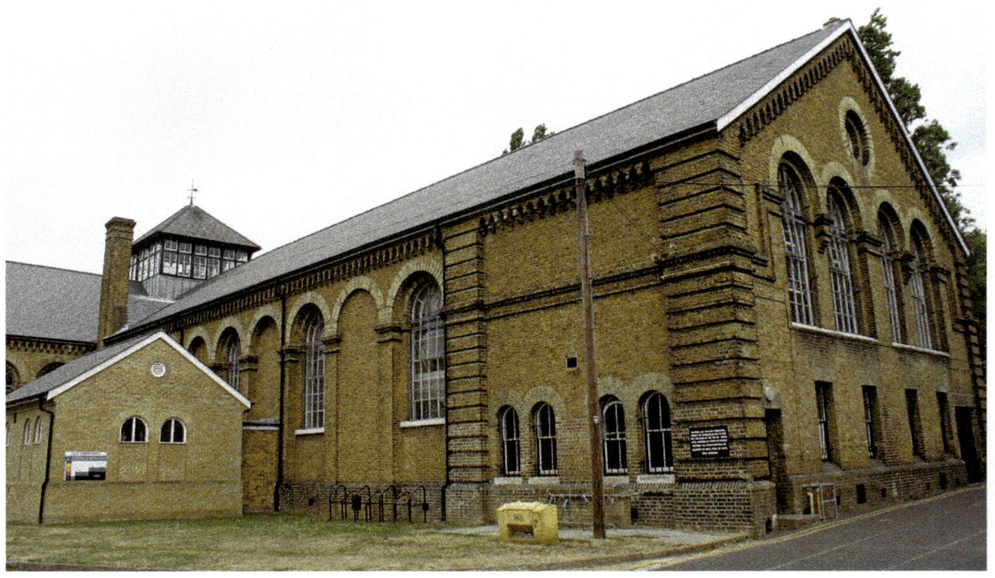

The Garrison Gymnasium.

Situated within the Inner Lines at Brompton, a convenient distance from the several barracks in Chatham, it was one of the first generation of gymnasiums purpose-built for the British Army and one of only two that survive today. As the gymnasium was a completely new venture for the army they had no fitness instructors to man it, so a number of non-commissioned officers from the various battalions of the garrison had to undergo a special training course to qualify them for the role. The gymnasium remains in use by the army today.

Officers' Mess, HMS 'Pembroke' Royal Navy Barracks

Probably the most recognisable and photographed group of buildings in the naval barracks. Designed by Sir Henry Pilkington and built in 1901 they housed accommodation and mess facilities for the commissioned officers. The grounds opposite contained a rose garden and croquet lawn as well as both hard and grass tennis courts for use in their leisure time. The University of Greenwich now use the buildings as office accommodation.

The Wardroom is located in the central block of buildings and was used for dining and recreation by all commissioned officers in the barracks above the rank of Midshipman. With its vaulted-beam ceiling, minstrels' gallery, oak-panelled walls and huge inglenook fireplace it is probably the grandest room in the barracks. The University of Greenwich now offer the Wardroom as an impressive venue for weddings and receptions catering for up to 180 guests.

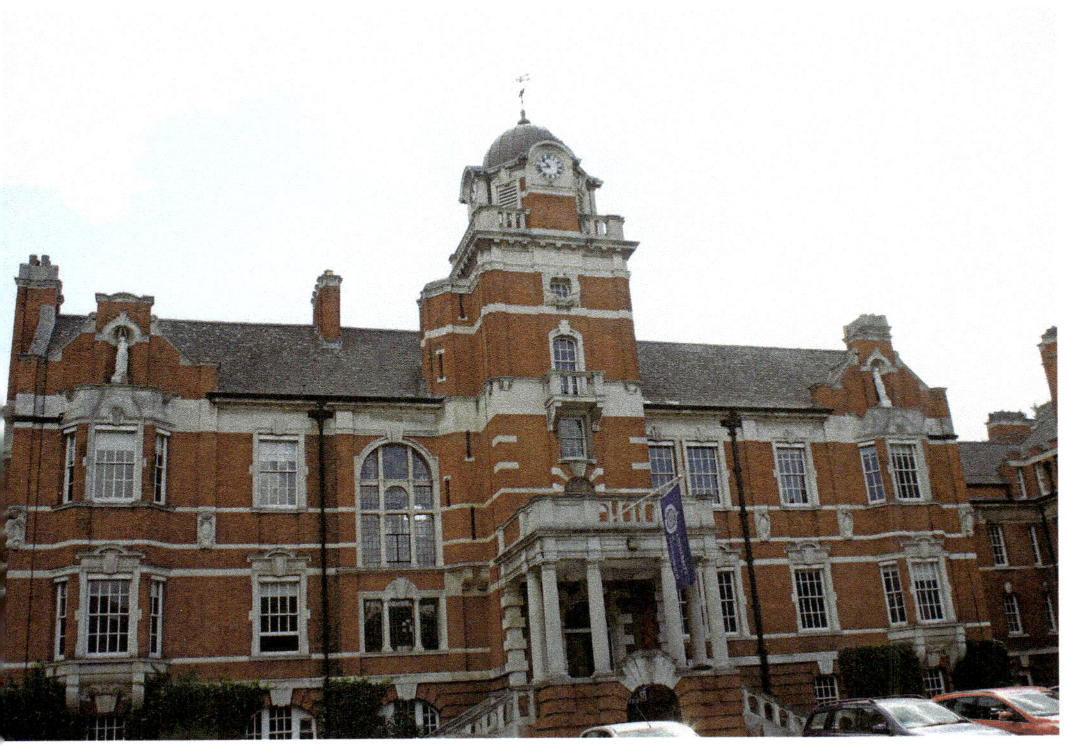

Royal Navy Barracks Officers' Mess.

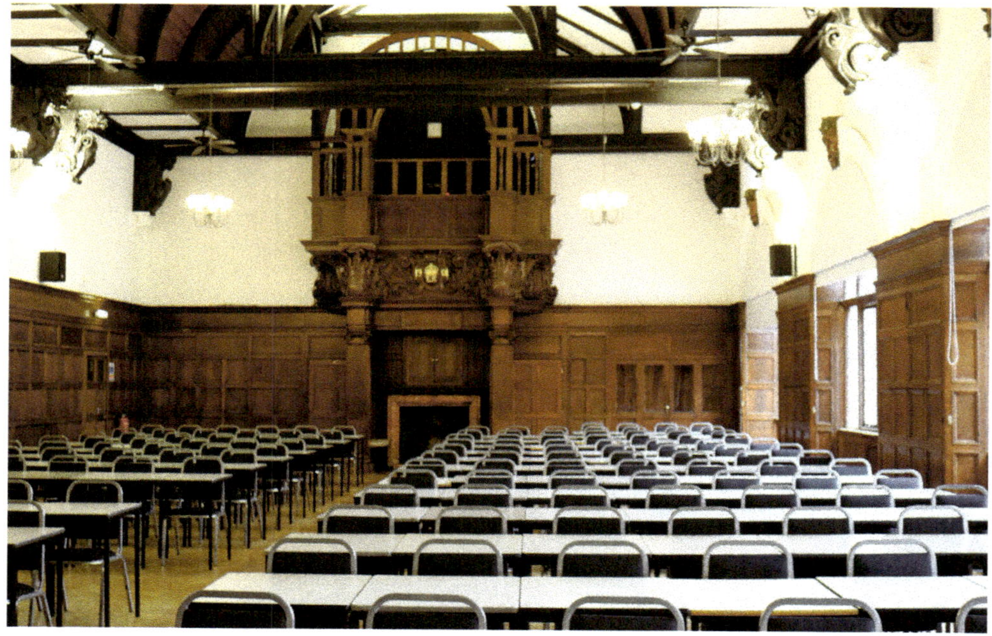

The Wardroom.

St George's Church, HMS 'Pembroke' Royal Navy Barracks

St George's Church was built in 1905 to serve the spiritual needs of the men from the Royal Navy's new barracks at Chatham. The church contains many memorials to the Royal Navy's ships and personnel and there are also two stained-glass windows, which

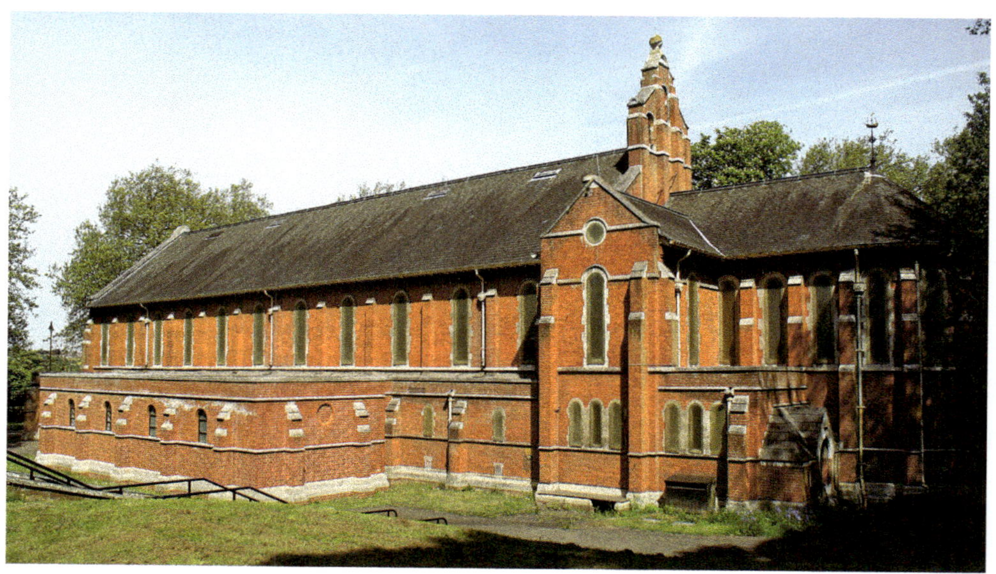

St George's Barrack Church.

were installed in 1954 as tribute from the navy's Nore Command to the Late King George VI. When the Royal Navy left Chatham in 1984 Medway Council took over the church and now hire it out as the St George's Centre for various indoor events and meetings. However, the memorials still remain inside together with a superb collection of naval artefacts.

Ravelin Building, Brompton Barracks

The Ravelin Building was built in 1906 to the design of Major E. C . S. Moore R. E. to house the Royal Engineers Electrical School. It was completed at a cost of £43,405. The Ravelin Building was the first building of the Royal Engineers to have a reinforced concrete structure. The establishment of the electrical school was an indication of the importance the Royal Engineers now attached to electrical skills for lighting, telegraphy and the detonation of explosives. The domed turrets at each corner of the building were designed to accommodate searchlights used in training. The building is now the home of the Royal Engineers Library and Museum.

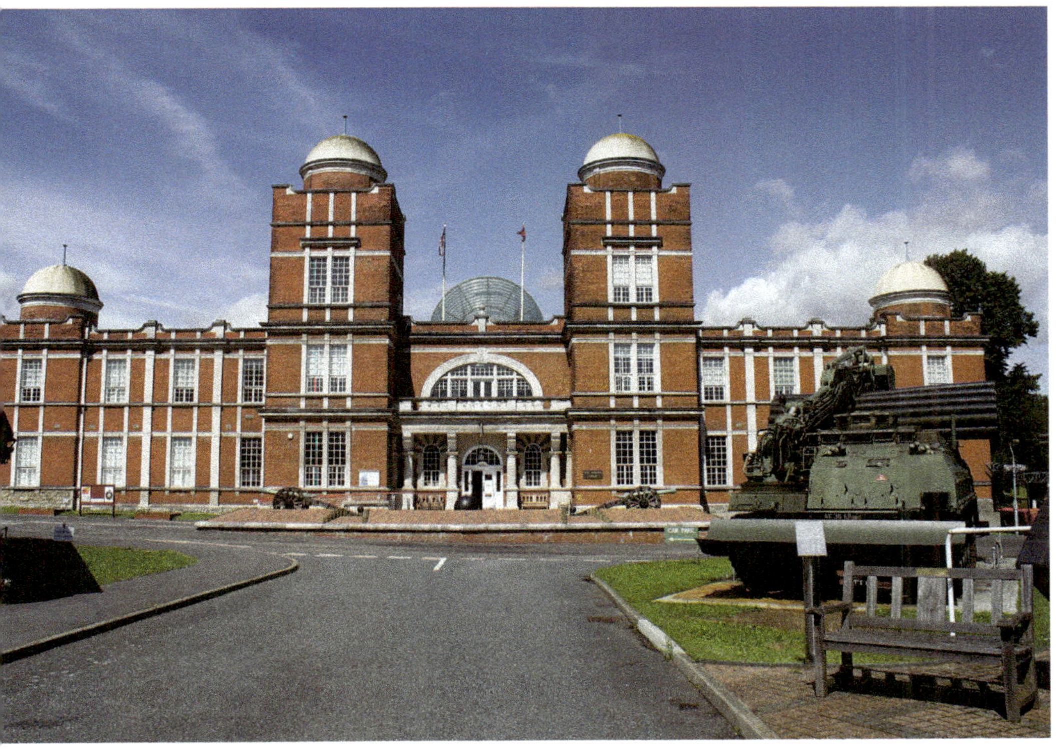

The Ravelin Building.

9. Memorials, Honours and Awards

As befits somewhere with such a long military history, Chatham has many memorials to those that have died in the service of their country.

French Prisoners of War Memorial

During the Napoleonic Wars French prisoners of war were incarcerated on board prison hulks moored at various naval ports and docks around the country. By 1799 over 25,000 prisoners were held in horrific conditions on board these ships including a large number held on the Medway in hulks moored in Short Reach and Gillingham Reach. Fatalities were high due to the overcrowded, insanitary environment and those that died at Chatham were buried in marshland on St Mary's Island and on, what was then, an island known as 'Prisoners' Bank'.

In the 1860s work began on land for the extension to the dockyard, which was to include the 'Prisoners' Bank' burial island off Gillingham Reach, so in 1869 the Admiralty ordered that these remains were to be removed and reinterred in the site on St Mary's Island. In total 711 skeletons were moved to what was by then known as the French Prisoner of

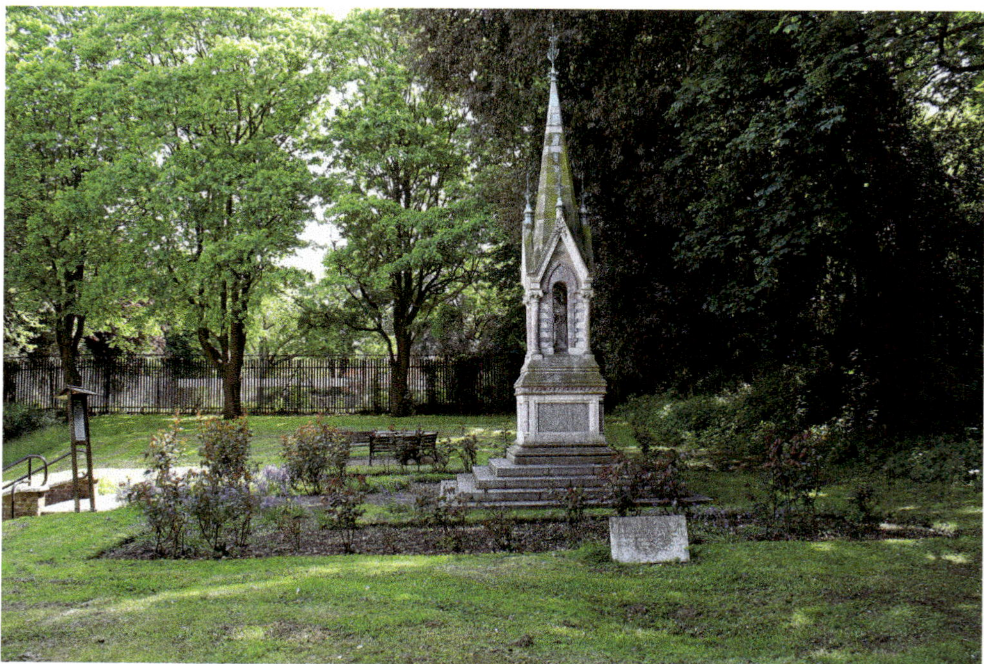

The French Prisoners of War Memorial at the St George's Centre.

War Cemetery. By this time relations with France had improved considerably and it was decided that a proper memorial should be erected on the site. The design of the memorial was approved by the French and was erected by some of the convict labour being used on the dockyard expansion. It was unveiled in 1871 and the Admiralty agreed to pay £5 per annum for its upkeep.

By 1903 the continued dockyard expansion work now threatened the St Mary's Island cemetery, so in 1904 the Admiralty ordered that all the remains be moved to a new site on high ground adjoining St George's Church at the Royal Naval Barracks. The transfer of the remains and the memorial was completed by 7 December 1904.

In 1991 the remains of a further 362 prisoners were discovered on St Mary's Island and these too were moved to the St George's Church site, which was now known as the St George's Centre following the departure of the Royal Navy from Chatham.

Fort Pitt Military Cemetery War Memorial

Largely unnoticed by the thousands who pass by it each day on the busy City Way road on the boundary of Rochester and Chatham is Fort Pitt Military Cemetery. The cemetery

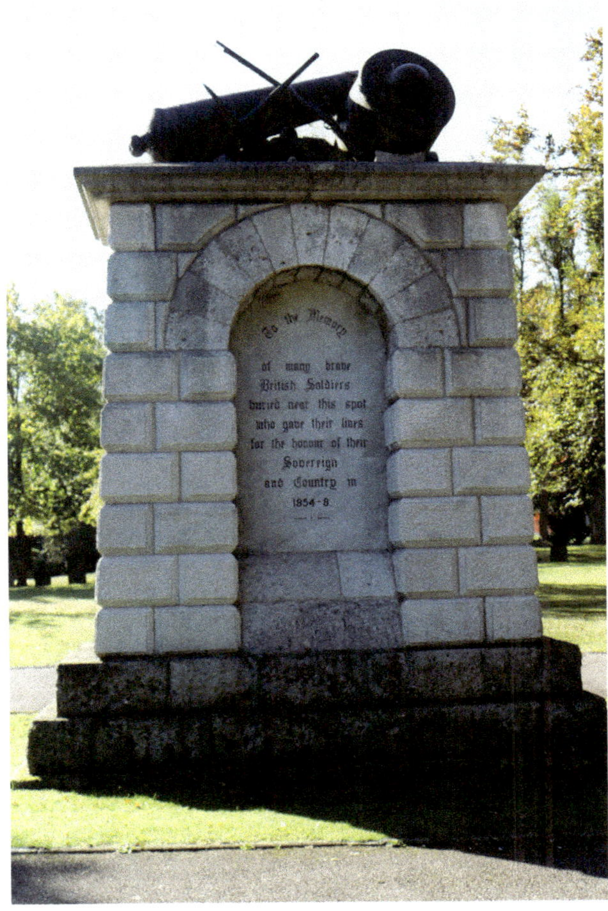

Fort Pitt Military Cemetery War Memorial.

was originally created in the mid-nineteenth century to serve the nearby military hospital. Within the entrance to the cemetery lies a large stone memorial dedicated to the memory of the soldiers of the British Army who lost their lives while in the service of their country between the years of 1854 and 1858 and whose remains are interred within the cemetery. The memorial was unveiled in December 1909 by General Charles Warren, Colonel-Commandant of the Royal Engineers.

Chatham Naval Memorial

Situated on the Great Lines overlooking the town the Chatham Naval Memorial was one of three identical memorials commissioned by an Admiralty committee after the First World War to commemorate those Royal Naval personnel that lost their lives during the war and had no known grave. The other Royal Navy Manning Ports at Portsmouth and Plymouth were chosen as the sites of the other two memorials. All three were designed by Sir Robert Lorimer with sculpture by Henry Poole. Each design is the same, with an obelisk of Portland stone surmounted by a copper sphere. The Chatham memorial, unveiled by the Prince of Wales in 1924, bears the names of over 8,500 sailors cast on bronze panels fixed to the buttresses of the monument. After the end of the Second World War the memorial was extended with surrounding walls on which are fixed fifty bronze panels with the names of 10,112 naval dead who perished at sea in that conflict. The extension was unveiled by the Duke of Edinburgh on 15 October 1952.

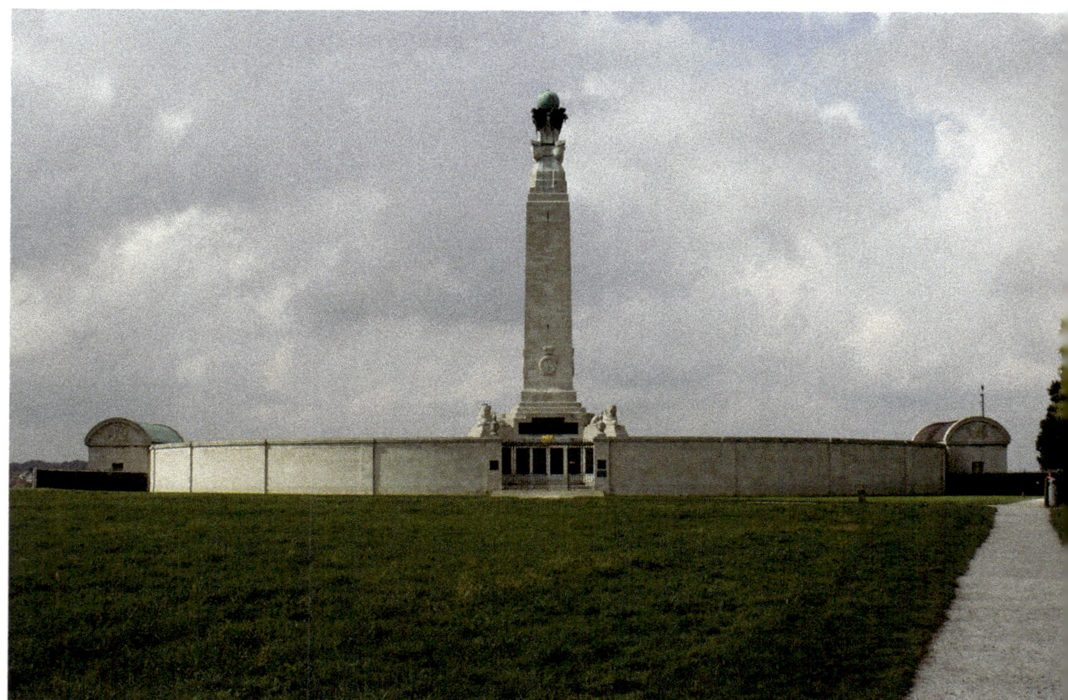

The Chatham Naval Memorial.

The people of the Medway Towns are rightly proud of their associations with the Armed Forces and that pride is reciprocated by the Services themselves. That mutual respect has been marked many times over the years and just two examples are:

Royal Engineers and The Freedom of the Borough of Gillingham

A Corps of Engineers was established in 1716, being given military rank in 1757. One of the first units was the 'Chatham Company'. The corps was responsible for the building of the fortifications of the Chatham Lines and for the great Victorian extension of the dockyard.

In 1812, the Royal Engineer Establishment was set up in Chatham and the following year the corps was renamed the Corps of Royal Sappers and Miners. In 1856, the soldiers of the Royal Sappers and Miners were absorbed into the Corps of Royal Engineers. The depot of the Royal School of Military Engineering was moved from Woolwich to Brompton Barracks and Chatham became the headquarters of the corps.

In 1953, in recognition of the long association of the Royal Engineers with the Medway Towns, the Freedom of the Borough of Gillingham was conferred upon the corps. The ceremony was conducted at Brompton Barracks on 10 September 1953 when the mayor of Gillingham presented the scroll in a ceremonial casket to the Colonel-Commandant of the Royal Engineers, General Sir Brian Hubert Robertson.

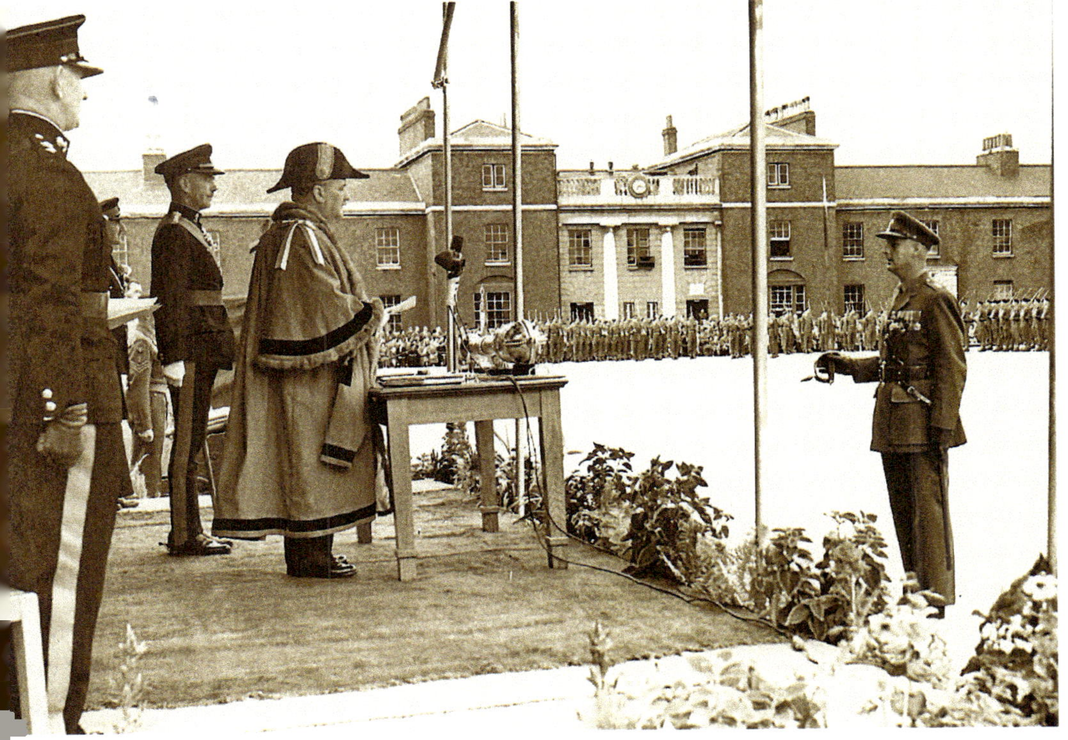

The officer commanding the parade asking permission from the mayor to march through the borough.

HMS *Chatham* and The Freedom of the Borough of Medway

Following the closure of the Royal Naval Base at Chatham in 1984 a decision was made to recognise the centuries-old association between the town and the navy by naming one of the new Type 22 frigates HMS *Chatham*. She was the fifteenth vessel of the Royal Navy to bear that name. She was built at Swan Hunter on Tyneside, launched in 1988 and commissioned in 1990. Although her home base was at Devonport she made a number visits to Chatham during her twenty-one-year career, the last one in 2010. HMS *Chatham* was decommissioned at Devonport on 10 February 2011 and on 12 February the ship's company exercised their historic right to the Freedom of the Borough of Medway and marched through Chatham with bayonets fixed accompanied by the Band of the Royal Marines.

HMS *Chatham*'s ship's bell, which had originally adorned the bridge of the vessel of the same name launched in 1912, was presented to the ship by the borough's predecessor, the City of Rochester Council, in 1990. It was re-presented to the mayor of Medway on 14 April 2011 and now resides in the St George's Centre, the former Royal Navy Barracks church.

The highest award a British serviceman can achieve for gallantry is the Victoria Cross. There have been several recipients of the VC with connections to Chatham.

Lieutenant Gerald Graham of the Royal Engineers was twenty-three years old when he won his VC on 18 June 1855 during the assault on the Redan at the Siege of Sebastopol during the Crimean War. He showed determined gallantry at the head of a ladder party at the assault on the Redan. British casualties during the assault were very high. Lieutenant Graham made repeated rescues of the wounded, under fire, bringing numerous wounded

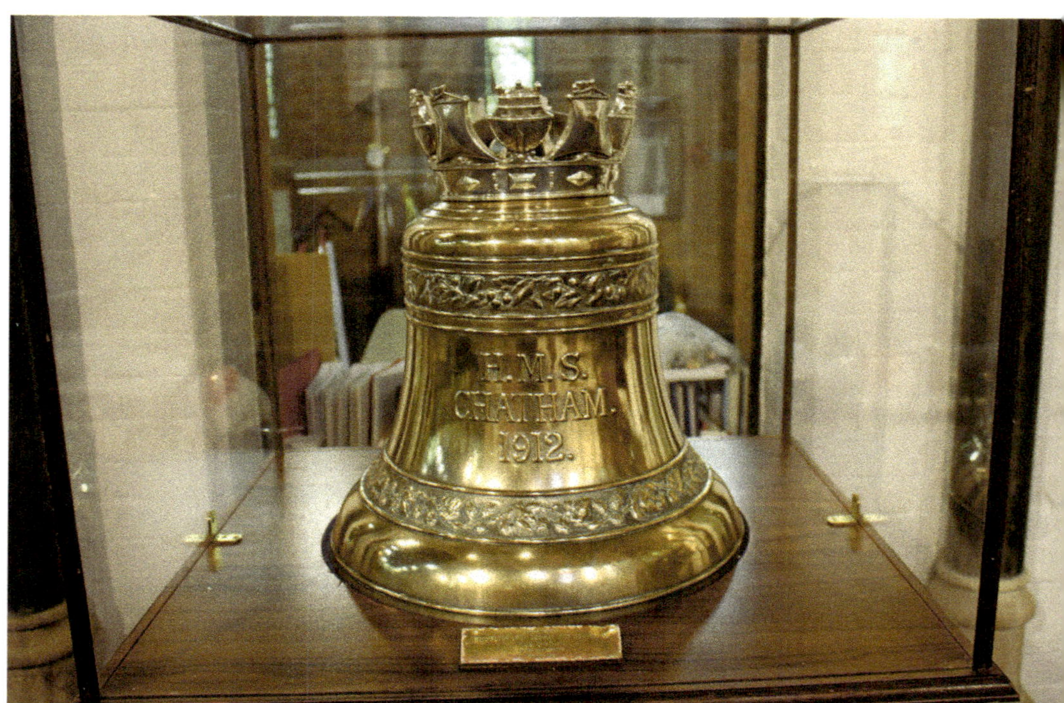

HMS *Chatham*'s ship's bell on display at the St George's Centre.

officers and men back to safety. The official citation of his VC commends Graham's 'devoted heroism'.

Graham was admitted to the Royal Military Academy at Woolwich in 1847 and completed his military training in the School of Military Engineering at Chatham. Graham was commissioned in the Royal Engineers as a Second Lieutenant on 19 June 1850. He rose to become Lieutenant-General Sir Gerald Graham VC GCB GCMG. On 10 March 1899 he was appointed Colonel-Commandant of the Corps of Royal Engineers. He died at Bideford in Devonshire on 17 December 1899. His VC is one of many awarded to Royal Engineers on display at the Royal Engineers Museum at Brompton.

Joseph Kellaway was twenty-nine years old and 3rd Boatswain aboard HMS *Wrangler* when he won his Victoria Cross on 31 August 1855 during the Crimean War. He was part of a five-man raiding party, commanded by the Mate, that had been ordered ashore to destroy a fishing station. They came under fire from a group of fifty Russian soldiers who then endeavoured to cut off their retreat. One of the raiding party was captured but the other four managed to make good with their escape until the Mate, Mr Odevaine, fell. Joseph Kellaway turned back attempting to rescue him while coming under heavy fire himself. The two men were surrounded by the Russians but continued to resist until they were forced to surrender and taken prisoner. However, despite his capture Kellaway was soon returned to England.

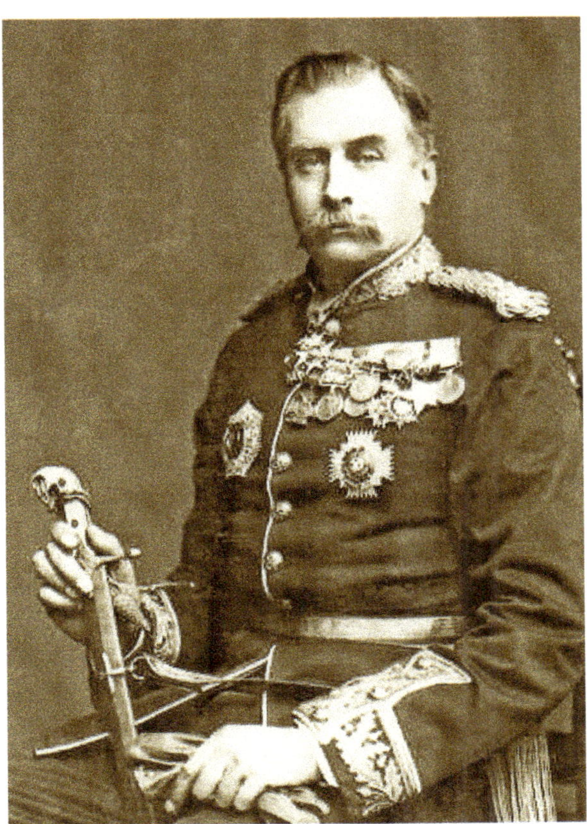

Lieutenant-General Gerald Graham VC GCB GCMG.

For his selfless efforts in attempting to rescue his commanding officer, Joseph Kellaway was awarded one of the first ever Victoria Crosses, which were presented personally by Queen Victoria at an investiture in Hyde Park, London, on 26 June 1857.

He was appointed Chief Boatswain at Chatham Dockyard in 1870 and continued to work and live there with his family until his death in 1880. He was buried at Maidstone Road Cemetery, Chatham.

One of the most famous recipients of the Victoria Cross was Lieutenant John Chard, whose heroic exploits at the Battle Rorke's Drift in the Anglo-Zulu War were immortalised by the actor Stanley Baker in the 1964 film *Zulu*.

John Chard was born in Plymouth in 1847 and educated at Plymouth and Cheltenham grammar schools before enrolling at the Royal Military Academy, Woolwich. He was commissioned as a lieutenant in the Royal Engineers in 1868 and spent the next two years training at the School of Military Engineering before being posted abroad in 1870. Chard returned to England in 1876 and was again posted to Chatham where he was assigned to the 5th Company, Royal Engineers.

In 1878, the 5th Company were sent to Natal Colony in southern Africa to assist with the invasion of the Zulu kingdom. On 22 January 1878 Chard found himself and his small group of sappers together with a company of the 2nd Battalion, 24th Regiment of Foot at the mission station at Rorke's Drift facing a force of 3,000–4,000 Zulus. As the senior officer on site Chard assumed command of the 140-man force, which included some thirty men sick or wounded at his disposal, and organised his defences

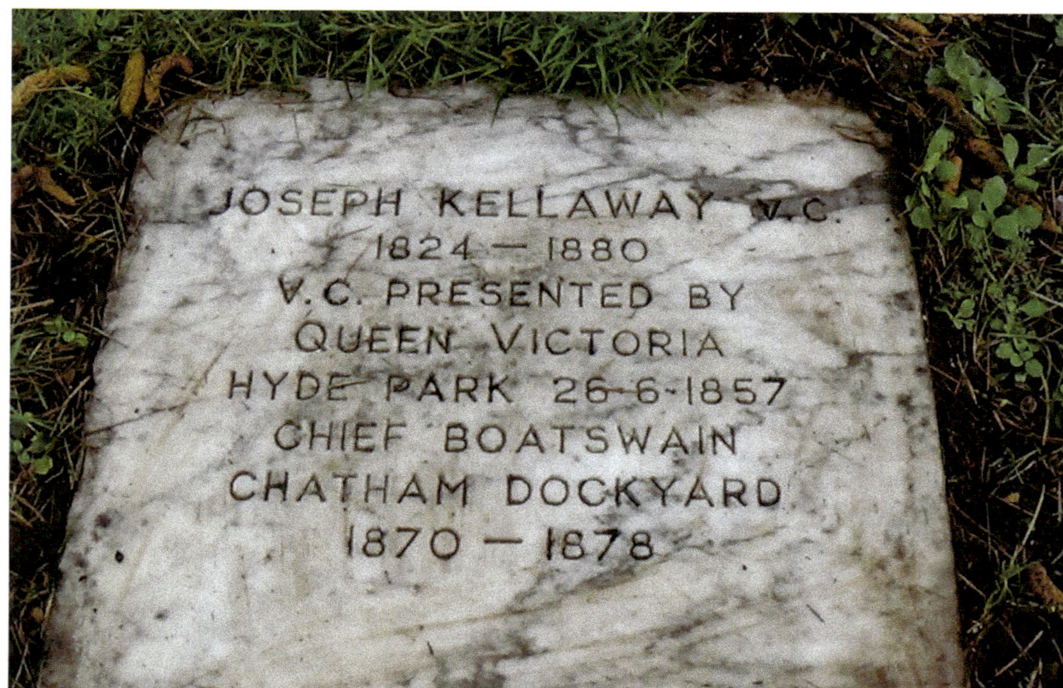

The grave of Joseph Kellaway VC in Maidstone Road Cemetery.

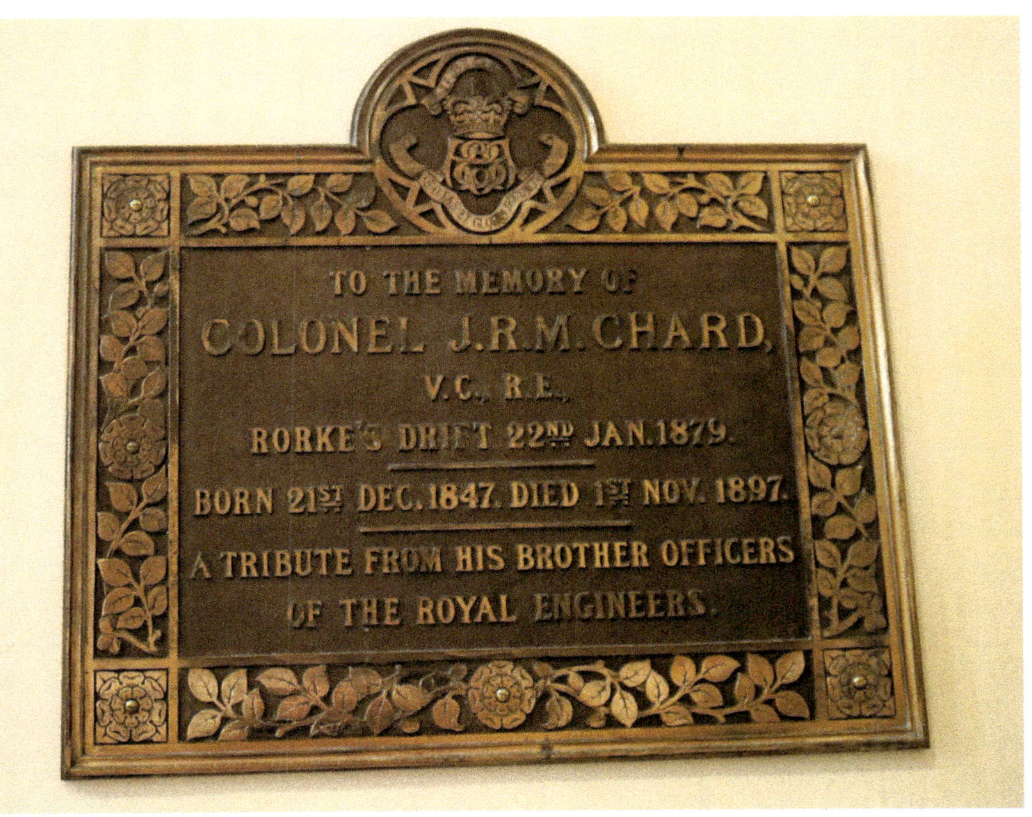

Plaque in memory of Colonel J. R. M. Chard VC in Rochester Cathedral.

accordingly. Despite being vastly outnumbered, Chard and his small force managed to repel several Zulu assaults, which carried on into the night. When dawn came the Zulus had withdrawn. For his part in the action Chard, along with ten other defenders, was awarded the Victoria Cross.

John Chard continued to serve with the army, rising to the rank of colonel, until 1897. He died in Somerset on 1 November 1897. There is a memorial to him in Rochester Cathedral and his Victoria Cross is now in the Lord Ashcroft Collection on display at the Imperial War Museum, London.

Bibliography

Gulvin, K. R., *Kent Home Guard* (North Kent Books, 1980).

Gulvin, K. R., *The Medway Forts* (Medway Historical Ordnance, 2007).

Kendall, P., *The Royal Engineers at Chatham 1750-2012* (English Heritage, 2012).

MacDougall, P., *The Chatham Dockyard Story* (Meresborough Books, 1987).

MacDougall, P., *Chatham Dockyard: The Rise and Fall of a Military Industrial Complex* (The History Press, 2012).

Presnail, J., *Chatham:The Story of a Dockyard Town* (The Corporation of Chatham, 1952).